And...

H

Andrew

24. ix. 93

SUCCESSFUL MODERN SALMON FLIES

SUCCESSFUL
MODERN
SALMON
FLIES

PETER MACKENZIE-PHILPS

BLANDFORD

This book is dedicated to my wife, Sue,
whom I have neglected for many years, never so much
as I have done in the last six months of work on this book.

By insulating me from many of the day-to-day distractions,
she has enabled me to concentrate on this task and,
by grinning at me when things went wrong,
has reminded me that life is for living.
(With a day's fishing from time to time!)

Series Editor: Jonathan Grimwood

First published in the UK 1989 by **Blandford Press**
An imprint of Cassell,
Artillery House, Artillery Row, London SW1P 1RT

Copyright © Peter Mackenzie-Philps 1989

Distributed in the United States by
Sterling Publishing Co., Inc.,
2 Park Avenue, New York, NY 10016

Distributed in Australia by
Capricorn Link (Australia) Pty Ltd,
PO Box 665, Lane Cove, NSW 2066

British Library Cataloguing in Publication Data
Mackenzie-Philps, Peter
Successful modern salmon flies.
1. Great Britain. Salmon. Fly fishing. Flies
I. Title
799.1'755

ISBN 0-7137-2053-0

Typeset by Graphicraft Typesetters Limited, Hong Kong

Printed in Portugal by Printer Portuguesa

CONTENTS

PREFACE

There are lots of books available today on the subject of salmon flies. The purpose of this Preface is to explain my motives in writing this book. I have been salmon fishing for forty years. I have not fished as often as I would like, but I have been fortunate in catching a few salmon. Not measured in thousands, but certainly a few hundred. Every one of these salmon has left me with the same thought – I caught it by accident. It must have been by accident because, for the life of me, I do not know why it took my fly.

I can cast as well as the next person. I have been teaching casting for twelve years and am now able to put my fly where I want it, whatever the problems of banks, trees, cliffs, fast currents and other obstacles to good presentation. I know *how* to get my fly out there, but I still do not know *why*.

Equally, I am still not sure what fly to put there. There are all sorts of rules dreamt up by anglers to dictate the choice of fly, none of which have ever been listened to or understood by salmon. On a bright day, does the salmon really prefer a bright fly? Then why did the man on the next beat catch a salmon with a black fly? The fact that I also caught a salmon with a bright fly only serves to confuse the issue. The same confusion exists with the size of the fly. Two anglers can catch salmon within a couple of minutes of each other, one using a size-12 fly and the other using an 8-cm (3-in) tube. Why?

I have set out to question the age-old rules, to look at some of the salmon flies that catch fish today. The same flies would have caught salmon a hundred years ago, but they were not invented then. Old salmon flies work today but the materials to make them, and the skills necessary to do so, are not now available in large enough measure.

We have had to change the materials used in fly-tying – flies have changed in shape, yet salmon are caught on things which would not have been recognized as flies a century ago. Man-made materials have an impact on flies used today, and this change accelerates as more materials are invented or discovered by enterprising fly-dressers.

This book is not intended just for the fly-dresser. Any salmon

6

angler will, I hope, find food for thought in the book and be able, after studying it, to ask in a tackle shop for the kind of flies wanted.

It is possible to buy flies in tackle shops all over the UK. By mail order it is possible to order flies from a fly-dresser anywhere in the British Isles. If you buy flies from two different sources, they may appear to be totally different, even though you gave the same name and size when ordering them. There will be such radical differences that you might not recognise the pattern as resembling the flies you wanted. The spread of flies in the colour section is designed to show how some of the differences can arise.

Above all, I set out in this book to make you think about the salmon, about what is going through its mind when it sees your fly. To think about what might make the difference in the mind of that fish between indifference to your offering, or a thrilling lunge that bends your rod and starts the reel screaming.

This book does not provide any rigid rules or irrevocable answers. I have none, and I know no one who has. We all, however, keep searching for the Holy Grail while we fish, yet at the same time we have the secret fear that if we ever do discover it, we shall spoil the thrill of the chase – the challenge would disappear, and we would give up salmon fishing altogether. The mysteries remain to baffle us, and to pose us the challenge. Long may it remain so.

Everything I say in this book is my personal opinion: it is not hard, proven fact. I do, however, have reasons for my personal opinions, and have thought through all I say on the subject of salmon fishing. I am fully conscious that we know little, and anyone who makes a firm statement about salmon is likely to be proved wrong in the next few minutes – not by the listener, but by the fish.

'You will never catch a salmon on that load of rubbish' – wallop.

'This fly is certain to raise a fish in this pool' – blank day.

I am sure you will be able to think of similar examples.

May I wish you tight lines and screaming reels. May you be lucky enough to catch lots of salmon by accident. If you ever truly find out why a salmon takes a fly, please will you let me know?

ACKNOWLEDGEMENTS

I have had unstinting help from many kind people while writing this book. The book started with the germ of an idea, and it would have remained stillborn without the generosity of time and trouble on the part of so many. Anglers and professional fly-dressers have sent me samples of their favourite flies and, in each case, I have mentioned them by name in the colour section. Help was forthcoming immediately from Ted Potter of the Fisheries Laboratory at Lowestoft, and from John Hislop and Godfrey Howard of the Marine Laboratory at Aberdeen. Without the chain of information that stemmed from their help, the book would have died at an early stage. In particular, Lieutenant Colonel Esmond Drury gave me time, advice, and encouragement that was all the more appreciated in view of his ill-health at the time he gave it. His kindness and help to me over the years is something I treasure.

I offer my thanks to all those kind people who have invited me fishing over the years on beats both large and small – shared happiness and experiences that have built up a fund of knowledge. If I could only remember all that knowledge at the same time I would perhaps be a good angler! But the memories will never fade.

I send my thanks to all the ghillies and boatmen who have helped me with a constant flow of advice and encouragement on days when nothing seemed to work – days I remember almost as well as the red-letter days when anything would work, and we tried to work out why. Without them our fishing would be a frustrating pastime indeed, and I have great admiration for their ability to turn the depression of a blank morning into the lightness of step with which we set off for the afternoon.

And finally to my publisher, Jonathan Grimwood, who had faith that I could produce this manuscript for him within the deadline. I am glad that I have managed it.

1.   WHAT IS A SALMON?

Talk to any normal salmon angler, or read any fishing magazine, and you are likely to be told that the salmon is the king of fish: a creature of magical beauty and strength, bravely overcoming incredible difficulty in returning to its birthplace to lay its eggs. All this is true. Laid as an egg in a depression in the gravel, fertilised by milt shed into the water beside those eggs, and covered up by the female thrashing its tail against gravel upstream of the redd – or nest – the little egg hatches in a few weeks to become a tender, tiny, alevin carrying its yolk-sac below it.

It wriggles its way out from the gravel, lives on the yolk until this is all consumed, and becomes a salmon parr. Perhaps 25 mm (1 in) long, the little parr eats almost anything that moves and that is smaller than itself, and grows over the next eighteen months to a length of perhaps 20 cm (8 in). In May of its second year it will turn silvery, and go down to the sea on a convenient flood, to disappear into the oceans. It is important to the little fish that it does turn silvery before it reaches the sea, as this is the natural camouflage of most fishes that inhabit the upper layers of the sea. The silvery colour reflects the colours around it.

We now know that salmon from the UK tend to go to an area of the North Atlantic. They follow an area of shallow water called the Wyville Thomson Ridge, running from the north of Scotland all the way to Greenland. Sticking up out of this ridge are, in turn, the Orkneys, the Shetlands, the Faeroes, Iceland, and Greenland. Off to the north of the ridge is Jan Mayen Island, and beyond this the sea bed drops off into the deeps of the Norwegian Basin. Nowhere in the oceanic feeding grounds of the UK salmon is the sea deeper than about 2,000 m (6,000 ft).

After a period that, for some reason, can vary from one to two – or even three – years, the salmon has grown to a considerable size, anywhere from perhaps 2.3 to 9 kg (5 to 20 lb). It then decides that the time is ripe for it to return to its parent river to spawn, and by some miracle of navigation it usually finds its birthplace – some say

9

by the smell of the water in its home river – to make its way upstream for the cycle to start all over again. After spawning, some of the adults die. Some, however, survive, and go all the way back to their ocean grounds to become even larger so that, on their second spawning run, they are the magnificent fish that make headlines in the fishing magazines. Fish of over 11.5 kg (25 lb) are usually on their second spawning run.

The navigation involved is incredible. As an example of this, consider fish that are heading for the Tweed. These approach the mouth of the river from the south. This seems illogical until one considers that, thousands of years ago, the Tweed was a tributary of the Rhine before the North Sea sank below the waves. Salmon coming from the direction of Iceland, therefore, follow the ancient bed of the Rhine, find the area where the Tweed once joined it, turn right, then follow the ancient bed of the Tweed running in a north-westerly direction. They actually come within a couple of miles of the UK coast in the area of Lincolnshire and follow the coast northwards, ignoring the mouth of the Humber as they go. They then ignore the mouth of the Tyne, and finally turn left into the Tweed after they have passed Holy Island.

How do they find their way? It has been suggested that they navigate by the stars, or by a form of built-in compass, following the magnetic variations in the earth's crust. But it might also be possible that they are following the old river valleys – the old contours where the rivers ran, and still might run, leaving a trace of fresh water. However fresh water is less dense than seawater, so currents of fresh water are nearer the surface, not running along the bed of the sea. Salmon do, though, seem to follow the courses of prehistoric rivers.

Talking to friends who are in contact with Northumberland drift-netters, I am reliably informed that, when a net is hung in the sea, the salmon will all be gilled between 2 and 5.5 m (6 and 18 ft) from the surface, with a fairly constant average figure of 3.7 m (12 ft). In other words, salmon on their way back to the Tweed swim at a fairly constant depth of around 3.7 m (12 ft). At this depth, colours are still clearly distinct and fresh water near the surface of the sea will, unless there is a great deal of wave action to mix it, be able to exert its influence on the salmon's incredible sense of smell.

This is one view of the salmon: a magnificent creature, causing wonderment, almost awe, in the minds of mere humans who cannot conceive its skills of navigation, its mating urge that overcomes all obstacles, and its power when played on rod and line.

I was talking in this vein one day on the bank of a Scottish river. My companion, an angler of vast experience, interrupted me to say: 'A salmon is only a big sea fish, which found out millions of years ago that it was safer to lay its eggs in fresh water, where there are fewer predators than there are in the sea. Think of a salmon as a bloody great herring, and you won't go far wrong.'

In front of us a salmon jumped in a shower of spray in the sunshine. How could a man be so heartless to even think like that? He wasn't heartless by nature. Yet he thought that a salmon was just a big sea fish that happened to spawn in rivers. He then went on to say that lampreys did the same, and no one thought that lampreys were magnificent! Eels did the same in reverse, migrating across the Atlantic to the Sargasso Sea, yet who thought that an eel was a magnificent creature? If anything, eels went further than salmon did – ten times further. All this talk of the magnificent creature, how brave it was, was all baloney, part of the mystique, the hype, to get anglers to crave the capture of a salmon so that they would pay huge sums of money to be able to do so!

He went on to ask me if I had ever caught a mackerel on a small rod and, yes, I had.

'How about that for power?' he asked.

I had to admit that, if a salmon had the same power as a mackerel, it would be impossible to land on salmon tackle. He then asked me if I thought that an old cock fish, almost chocolate brown in colour with a big kype, was as magnificent in appearance as a silvery-blue fresh-run fish just off the tide. No, I had to admit that I did not regard the old, stale, fish with quite the same reverence as I did a silvery springer.

'There you are' he said. 'It's the same fish, only a couple of months in the river makes such a difference to your outlook. Why should you think that the fresh fish is so magnificent and the stale cock is an ugly brute to be put back? All you are thinking about is your stomach – one will be good to eat, the other will taste like blotting-paper, even if it is smoked.'

I think back to that conversation often. It didn't finish there, of

course, as we went on to discuss the instincts that drive a salmon –
no power of thought, just instincts, mainly predatory or mating and
at times one is more powerful than the other. Few other instincts
seem to matter, he went on to say, except the overall one of self-
preservation.

Later that day I watched that man fishing. He did so with total
dedication. He fished in a half-crouch, the epitome of the hunter,
totally absorbed in what he was doing. Mentally he was not standing
on the bank – his brain was fixed underwater where his fly was,
working out how deep it was, how fast it was moving, what impression it gave as it flickered in and out of the currents.

I cannot bring myself to believe that a salmon is 'just a bloody
great herring', although I have come to agree with some of the views
that particular man held about what goes through a salmon's mind
when it sees my fly. I still look at a salmon I have just killed with a
mixture of awe and gratitude, sadness and joy, and I am usually still
shaking with the thrill of battle ten minutes afterwards.

I had that conversation perhaps twenty years ago. I caught one
salmon that day, and my companion caught four. 'You got that one
by accident,' he said. Knowing what I know now, or what I think I
know now, I am inclined to believe him.

I rather think that most salmon caught on rod and line today are
caught by accident. A happy accident, perhaps, but still an accident.
You don't agree? Are you telling me that you can lay your hand on
your heart and say that you caught your last salmon by sheer skill?
Have you never flogged away for a week without a pull, and on the
Saturday afternoon your fly has suddenly stopped with a thump.
You look upwards and say, 'Thank you, God, now don't let it get
off!' If it was sheer skill, why bother thanking Him? You thank Him
for the happy accident that put your fly in front of a salmon, which –
at that very moment – was stupid enough to grab it. Five minutes
earlier, or five minutes later, your fly could well have been totally
ignored. And that, surely, is much of the thrill of salmon fishing.

2. WHY DID THAT BEAUTIFUL FISH TAKE MY FLY?

We could argue for a long time whether a salmon is a freshwater fish that goes to sea because there is not enough food for it in the river of its birth, or whether it is a sea fish that enters fresh water to spawn. Most salmon anglers like to think of the salmon as a freshwater fish they are trying to catch in its home environment. Certainly, there is not enough food in a river to allow a salmon to grow at the rate it does while at sea. To grow from a parr weighing at the most fifty or so grams to a grilse weighing perhaps 2.75 or 3 kg (6 or 7 lb) in the space of twelve to fourteen months must involve intensive feeding. Such intensive feeding cannot be finicky – the salmon must be aggressively omnivorous, eating anything that moves within reach.

We are told that salmon, when entering fresh water, stop feeding. It has been proved, by analysis of stomach contents of Atlantic salmon on the eastern seaboard of North America (Jones, 1959) that sexually-maturing salmon generally cease feeding even before entering freshwater from the sea. Yet I have examined the stomach of a salmon netted at the mouth of the Tweed and found a sand-eel in it – just one, but it was there, and not that many hours old.

So, if all we are told is true, why does a salmon take a fly, spinner, prawn, or worm when it is offered in such hope by the angler? Hugh Falkus, in his fascinating book, *Salmon Fishing*, lists the following reasons for a salmon taking a fly, in a rough order of likelihood:

1. Feeding habit.
2. Aggression.
3. Inducement.
4. Curiosity.
5. Irritation.
6. Playfulness.

Let us consider some of these reasons as listed by Hugh. Suppose you were sitting in a deckchair on a nice sunny day, totally at peace with the world, perhaps with the Sunday paper over your face. Suddenly you become aware of the whining of a wasp near your head. You can decide to ignore it – it will go away. You may do this for some minutes, but there will come a time when you swipe at it with the paper. You have hands and can do this. A salmon has no hands, and so cannot swipe at anything. But it can snap at something with its mouth, and often does.

It is tempting to assume that the salmon snatching at your fly does so from a similar motive to your irritation or aggression. But was the motive similar? Might the motive not be a feeding habit reasserting itself? If a salmon grabs at food-forms in the sea we call it feeding. When it does the same in a river, do we call it aggression or irritation? Personally I am not convinced – I think it is still the feeding habit, and that we are wrong to try to credit the salmon with a human emotion like aggression or irritation.

I have lain in my bath staring at the ceiling for inspiration, and tried to imagine that I was a little salmon smolt, heading out of the estuary into the open sea. I reflected that I may have seen my first sand-eel, and grabbed it. It tasted nice, so I started to eat other sand-eels. Later on, I came across my first baby herring and snapped at that, with the same result. In short, everything had to be tried to see if it was edible, and most creatures were. So the adult salmon arrives back in its home river, sees something strange flickering across the pool above its head, and grabs it. I do not think it matters all that much that the colour may be wrong for a baby herring – if it looks like a little fish and moves like a little fish, it probably is a little fish, whatever colour it is.

What about the salmon that refuses the fly for twenty casts and then wallops it on the twenty-first? Irritation is a tempting thought, but I feel it is more logical to think that it is still the feeding habit that just took some time to trigger – like the small boy, briefed by Mum to accept only one of Auntie's chocolate biscuits, or else. If Auntie presses him for long enough, he will crack and take a second, and to hell with what Mum will say on the way home! Or the man who gave up smoking a year ago, and is offered a cigarette for the tenth time at a Christmas party. He refused the first nine offerings, but he took the tenth. He knows it is bad for him, and that he shouldn't do it, yet he cracked just like the small boy. Why should it not be equally true that the salmon knows it shouldn't eat in fresh water, but will crack if offered food, or what looks like food? Why should we then think it is aggression when all it is is a lack of willpower, and a reassertion of the feeding urge? Before somebody jumps on me and tells me that salmon do not stop feeding in fresh water because of willpower, let me say straight away that it is perhaps the temporary breakdown of physiological conditioning not to feed. Lack of willpower is a human frailty from which fish do not suffer.

Inducement is another of Hugh's possible reasons. Could this not be explained in just the same way as in the previous paragraph? Offer someone something often enough, and you can induce them to take it. But I suggest that the salmon still takes it as food, like the small boy with the second chocolate biscuit.

Curiosity can be a motive for a salmon to take a fly into its mouth. But why is it curious? Is it thinking, 'What is that?' or is it thinking, 'Is that edible?' When that salmon first went to sea as a smolt, it must have been curious when it saw its first shrimp, its first herring fry, its first sand-eel, or whatever, and it learned pretty quickly that if something moved it was almost certain to be edible. So why should we attribute the spirit of curiosity to a salmon? Surely it is more logical to credit salmon with the feeding urge only, instead of the motive of curiosity.

Playfulness is dealt with by Hugh in giving a lovely example of a fish twirling around under a worm – almost blowing bubbles with it. I have never seen this for myself, and am thus not qualified to comment. But children play with bubble-gum in the Western world. In starving Africa, children would eat the same bubble-gum without playing with it. At dinner parties I have seen grown men and women playing with a grape while engaged in a conversation, or chasing a piece of cheese round a plate. I have also seen young men, who should have known better, throwing bread rolls at each other. These are examples of humans playing with food instead of just sticking it in their mouths for the nourishment it contains. I suppose salmon could do the same if they were so minded. I would believe the playfulness motive a lot more if someone could tell me of salmon playing with stones they picked off the bottom, or draping each other with seaweed! In the meantime, I am prepared to believe that they might play with food for a while before eating it, but that they intend to eat it eventually!

It is said that if something is repeated often enough it will be believed, so how about this example: *salmon do not feed once they enter fresh water* – period. Oh no? What about the salmon I saw rise to an olive – covered without thought with a size-14 Greenwell's Glory – which rose like a huge trout and took it while my jaw dropped with a mixture of elation and horror? The fact that it ran me ragged and then broke me makes no difference. That salmon thought it was eating an olive, of that I am certain.

I was lying on a high rock one day, worming for salmon. I could see every detail of the pool below me in the bright sunshine. I trundled my bunch of worms towards a salmon, and saw it move forward 30 cm (1 ft) or so to take it. My companion, an elderly and vastly-experienced angler, told me not to strike but to wait until the fish took the worms back to its lie. I waited and waited. The salmon did not move. Suddenly, after perhaps fifteen seconds, it spat that bunch of worms out so violently that it shot perhaps 60 cm (2 ft) upstream against the current. Looking at the bunch of worms, they had been squeezed so that the empty skins were all that were left. I must admit that that salmon did not intend to eat those worms, but I am certain that it enjoyed a drink of worm juice, and to my mind that is still eating.

I think, too, of the last salmon I caught this year, which had the treble of the tube fly stuck right at the back of its throat. I am happy with the thought that the salmon intended to eat my fly – there is no other possible reason for the hook to have gone so far down. I am not, therefore, prepared to believe that *salmon do not feed once they are in fresh water*. I am prepared to believe that *most salmon* do not feed while they are in fresh water. I am prepared to believe that salmon do not feed for *most of the time* they are in fresh water. Equally, I am convinced that salmon do, from time to time, forget that they are *not supposed to feed* in fresh water, and take something into their mouths.

In other words, it is my humble opinion that salmon *do* think they are feeding when they take a salmon fly. (Or when they take a Devon, a Rappala, a Kynoch Killer, a Toby, a bunch of worms, a prawn, or whatever.) For some reason – not fully understood – a salmon that has recently been moving is more likely to have its reflexes triggered by a fly than is a somnolent fish. A fish just off the tide, stopping for its first rest in the river, seems to be more prone than any other to take a fly – perhaps because the feeding memory is so recent?

If a salmon *thinks* it is eating when it takes my fly, will I not maximise my chances of triggering this instinctive reaction if I make a conscious endeavour to make my fly look like some form of food the salmon will recognise? After all, spinners and spinning lures are deliberately designed to look like little fish – so why should salmon flies be designed by hunch, because some human being likes the pretty colours?

We could, of course, believe that, if a salmon fly is moving, the fish will think it is edible. If it moves it must be food. If we believe that, we should also believe that the pattern of fly is totally immaterial and, within reason, that the size of fly is also immaterial. There are enough examples of fish taking widely-differing sizes and colours of fly within a few minutes of each other for this perhaps to be true. But if we really believe this, we would not bother at all with different colours or sizes of fly. We would stick any old thing on the end and make it move. Most of us would not have the courage to fish like this, especially if we had just spent a month's pay for a week on a salmon river!

Most of us have to have great faith in the fly we fish so diligently through a salmon pool. If the word goes around that Prince Charles caught three fish in one afternoon on a Munro Killer, the tackle shops for fifty miles around are cleaned out of Munro Killers within hours. The purchasers will all be fishing with just that little bit more confidence than they did the day before when they were using Hairy Marys. It would be a strong-minded cynic who would state that the fish could not tell the difference.

Let us analyse the motives in the mind of the person who invents a salmon fly. They are sitting at their fly-tying vice, putting a hook in

17

the vice jaws. They will almost certainly reach for a spool of black thread, because most salmon flies are tied with black thread! They will then tie in a tail, body material, ribbing, hackle, and wings in colours of their choice, acting on hunch. When the fly is finished, they will try to look at it with a critical eye, and will form the impression that it 'looks fishy' or it doesn't. It is rather like someone trying to tie an imitation of a pond olive who has never in their life seen an upwinged fly of any kind – fumbling in the dark, surely.

Would we not optimise the chance of a salmon grabbing our fly if we were to set out deliberately to imitate the food-forms the salmon ate in such abundance in the ocean (having the size, shape, colour, outline, or suggestion of all of these, correct) then to fish that fly with the correct movement for that food-form? By doing this would we not be removing any curiosity element in the mind of the salmon, if there is one, causing the salmon to take the fly with more confidence? Might this also give anglers more confidence that they were trying to fool a fish into taking – doing something positive and constructive – instead of attaching a pattern that represents nothing in nature, and hoping that a fish will be foolish enough to have a go at it when it swims smoothly across the currents of a salmon pool time after time?

Let us look first at the flies that are catching most salmon today. What are the flies reposing in thousands of flyboxes and hundreds of tackle-shop trays?

3. SHUT YOUR EYES AND CHOOSE ME A FLY FROM THAT BOX

'There is a fish behind that rock. If it's a taker, you will catch it. If it's not, you are wasting your time.' How often have you heard that sort of statement, uttered with the authority of one who has read it on stone tablets? The fact that the behaviour of the salmon often *seems* to bear out the statement is reason enough for the average angler to believe it utterly.

Most of us do not spend enough time fishing for salmon. If we are lucky, we spend a couple of weeks a year on the banks of salmon rivers. If we are very rich indeed, we may spend four, or even six weeks a year salmon fishing. If we are only an average salmon angler, our time will be more likely one week or less each year. There are often good reasons for the time during that week to be divided between fishing and some other activity, like shopping and sightseeing with the family, being flooded off the river, or there being so little water that we feel that it is a waste of time even trying to catch a fish.

The average angler, therefore, is prey to the spread of disinformation in books, magazine articles, and talk at the bar. It is not intended to be disinformation, of course, and much of it is leavened with a goodly measure of experience and common sense, but salmon fishing does seem to be a sport prone to a high content of old wives' tales:

'the brighter the day, the brighter the fly';
'the faster the current, the bigger the fly';
'that pattern works on the Conon, but not here'.

These are examples of beliefs, handed down from generation to generation of salmon anglers, perhaps in the hope of giving confi-

19

dence in one's fly, and reducing the bewilderment of choice of what to tie on the end before flogging away for hour after hour. If we have some rules to follow, we will perhaps fish more doggedly, and for longer, and thus will inevitably catch more. So the rules do serve a purpose – and they are not necessarily wrong: there is a mathematical probability that they will be right for half the time! Faced with this lack of hard facts, the average angler turns to books, of which there is a bewildering array on the subject of salmon. Let us choose just two, and see what they say.

Arthur Oglesby, a man for whom I have the highest respect and who has caught more salmon that I have 'had hot dinners', has written many books on fishing. I chose one at random from my shelves – *Salmon* – and culled the following quotations from it:

> It is largely a matter of choice which is used . . . . It is my fancy, and purely a fancy, that the smaller we make our flies, the less important the colour seems to be . . . . Nevertheless, I think the angler should have an eye for colour, and the fly should be dangled in the water, and inspected against the river bed, so that the angler can assess its appearance and decide whether it appears to fall in line with its new environment.

Being an honest man, Arthur has to say, in effect, that you choose a fly from your box acting more or less on hunch, and stick it in the water to see if it looks right. If you *feel* happy with it, you fish with as much confidence as you need to flog away for hours until you happen to come across a 'taker'. But even Arthur cannot define what 'looks right'.

Hugh Falkus, in his book, *Salmon Fishing*, goes into some detail on the choice of fly. After discussing the size needed for the fly to swim at a certain depth, he says:

> If you seek guidance from some gnomic wisdom as 'A bright fly for a bright sky, a dark fly for a dark lie', or vice versa – or from some other homespun maxim stitched in runes – select only those patterns that seem to fit your particular bill . . . . You have now short-listed three or four possibles. Tip these into your hat, and

pick one out . . . . Choice of fly boils down to what was written a century ago. There is no magic substitute for experience. Experience merely reduces the number of flies you tip into your hat. When you are very experienced, you may not need to tip in any at all.

What Hugh is really saying in that last sentence is, I suspect, that when you have been salmon fishing for many years you will merely react quicker to hunch, and thus will have become more hidebound in your choice of fly! And I have to say that Hugh's book is a total fascination for me, and for many others I have spoken to.

When men of the experience of these two cannot be more definite than this on the choice of fly, what hope is there for the rest of us? They have fished all over the world during their lifetimes, and they are no nearer firm rules than are any of us. Neither of them can say, for instance, that if the wind is in the west, the barometric pressure x millibars, the river is at 60 cm (2 ft) on the gauge, and the water is clear in April, you should fish a fly size 6, coloured black and orange!

However experienced the salmon angler we were to question at the riverside, we would find that he had done exactly as Arthur and Hugh suggested. Staring into his flybox with a certain glazed look, he will have chosen a fly by pure hunch. It just happened to catch his eye and look right for the moment. It might be the fly on which he caught fish yesterday, or the pattern on which he caught his first-ever salmon. In short, he will have used a kind of hunter's instinct, rather than a set of exact scientific rules. His ghillie or boatman, looking into the same box of flies, might well choose an altogether different fly, or even reject the lot and offer one from his hat. While the ghillie will have a great breadth of experience on that water, he will be no more scientific than the visiting angler. The trouble with salmon fishing is that they could both be right – widely-differing flies can catch fish on the same day.

Ghillies tend to be hidebound by tradition. I once gave some patterns to an angler and asked him to test them for me. On his return I eagerly asked him if they had worked, only to be told that the ghillie would not let him use them, but had insisted that he fish with the flies 'which always work here'. The ghillie, of course, thought that he was doing his angler a favour by maximising his chances of catching fish. He perhaps thought that he was also maximising his chances of a tip, but I am sure that this was a secondary consideration – fish on the bank are more important than money to many of the ghillies I have met.

There is also the fear of wasting time trying patterns that might not work. Salmon fishing is today so expensive that time spent experimenting is almost regarded as a waste of money. This fear extends into the tackle shop, reflected in the choice of salmon flies in the trays on the counter, which will only be the tried and trusted favourites. I do not know a tackle dealer brave enough to stock patterns that *might* work. The dealer must be able to say 'That's a grand fly' about any of the patterns on offer, so that the purchaser goes away with a buoyant step and the conviction of being able to catch a bagful!

Let us now take a slightly different tack. Suppose we could ask salmon anglers all over Scotland which fly they caught their salmon on. A survey of this kind would reveal all, but I can think of no way of doing it with any accuracy. However, river reports are published every month in *Trout and Salmon* magazine, and quite a few of these do carry details of successful flies. I have found those by Rogie to be the most helpful, and he seems to cover many of the northerly rivers.

I started by analysing the river reports for two years – 1983 and 1987. I listed every single fly mentioned, and added up the number of times each fly was quoted. While I found the answers fascinating, I fully realise that there is a strong possibility that most salmon caught in Scotland are not caught on fly but on a worm, bunch of worms, a spinner, or bait of some kind. Ignoring that, I ended up with a list of flies that had been successful in catching salmon, and the list of the ten most popular patterns for each year looks like Table 1.

Let me say straight away that this list cannot be regarded as anything other than a very rough guide. It is quite possible that, for instance, every time a Willie Gunn is mentioned in the river reports it is the tube-fly version that is meant. And this reservation could be applied to any of the patterns mentioned. I feel, however, that

Table 1   The ten most popular fly patterns, 1983 and 1987.

1983	%	1987	%
Stoat's Tail	15.5	Tubes or Waddingtons	19.3
Tubes or Waddingtons	14.5	Willie Gunn	13.7
Munro Killer	9.1	Munro Killer	13.0
Shrimp flies, various	8.5	Shrimp flies, various	9.3
Willie Gunn	5.6	Stoat's Tail	8.4
Collie Dog	4.6	Garry Dog	4.6
Hairy Mary	4.2	Tadpole	4.3
Blue Charm }		Hairy Mary	3.7
Tosh }	3.8	Collie Dog	2.8
Silver Stoat	2.8	Tosh	2.5

realising that it is only a guide, a few interesting observations can be made with some certainty.

First, salmon anglers are *not* adventurous in their choice of fly. The same patterns crop up, in roughly the same order, four years apart. So where are the new patterns? Or are there any new patterns? I cannot believe that, with the spread of fly-tying as rapid as it is, salmon anglers are not inventing new patterns as are their rainbow-trout-angling counterparts. I think that the answer must be that new patterns are just not used except by their inventors, due to the inbuilt dread by the salmon angler that any experimentation on fly patterns might cost fish. It is far better to stick to the tried and tested patterns – and for the last four years it seems that the angler has done just that.

However, Mr Munro invented the Munro Killer, and it became rightly popular. It seems also to be gaining in popularity. So some anglers who would not have used it in 1983 used it in 1987. Fashion? Publicity? Word-of-mouth? River reports? For whatever reason, fashions in salmon flies change slowly – but change they do, or we should all still be using the huge meat-hooks of the last century, fully dressed with exotic feathers.

To look at the table again, it could be suggested that 13 per cent of salmon were caught on a Munro Killer in 1987 because 13 per cent of anglers were using Munro Killers. If we accept that, we accept that it makes no difference to the salmon what fly is offered. The fish took the fly that was there in front of them, whatever it

23

was. Surely if we accepted that we would have only one pattern in our flyboxes, and the tackle trade would die. We have to believe that some change in the colouring, style, or size of our fly is going to make a difference, or we would not fish with a fly at all.

Second, there seems to be a rising popularity in the use of tubes and Waddingtons. From my own observations there seems little doubt of this. The tube can be made of brass for heavy spring and autumn fishing, or a 6-mm (¼-in) long piece of plastic tubing from a ball-point pen with six black hairs on it for the height of summer – at each extreme it offers one big advantage in the mind of the angler: the treble hook that increases the chance of a good hook-hold. I think it would be correct to say that, these days, few salmon anglers fish with single hooks on a regular basis (dapping flies excluded – salmon caught on the dap are usually a happy accident on a day of sea-trout fishing).

Third, the only fly that has dropped out of the top ten, the Blue Charm, is also the only fly with a feather wing. It is most significant that in 1983 only one of the top ten patterns had a feather wing, and in 1987 not one of the top ten is other than a hair-wing pattern. Actually in eleventh, twelfth, and thirteenth places for 1987, at less than 2 per cent each, are three feather-wing patterns: the Teal Blue and Silver, the General Practitioner, and the Blue Charm. The reduction in popularity of feather-wing patterns cannot be caused by the difficulty many fly-dressers have with winging – I feel it is more likely that anglers have been persuaded by the 'mobile in the water giving an impression of life' theory of the *aficionados* of hair-wings.

Does the pattern or style of the fly really make a difference? I believe that it does make a difference to the spirit of the angler. There is a sensuous pleasure to be had by looking into a flybox of nicely-dressed salmon flies. To the fish, I am not at all sure. Two stories might illustrate the dilemma.

I was fishing many years ago on a bitterly cold March day on the River Tyne. I was using a slow sinking line and a 5-cm (2-in) tube fly. There were four other anglers on the beat. One was using a fast-sinker with an 8-cm (3-in) tube fly. One was using a Toby. One was using a wooden Devon. Last, there was my old fishing pal, who was using a floating line and a fly tied on a double hook, size 4. At about 12 o'clock my old friend suggested that the river was dead, we were wasting our time, and that it was time for hot soup. I told him that I had just realised that the birds were singing, and that I would fish for a little while longer. At that moment I hooked a fish that turned out to be a magnificent 11 kg (24 lb). Immediately I suggested that he went back to the head of the pool to try again, which he did. Second cast, and he was into a fish. I looked down the river while I was playing mine, and saw to my amazement that the other three anglers were also playing fish over the half mile of the beat. Analysing the incident afterwards, it was clear that this could not have been a shoal of fish having a rest – shoals of salmon are not half-a-mile long, at least not on the Tyne in those days. Something caused a proportion of the salmon in the river to take, and it did not seem to matter what it was in front of them at the time the urge came upon them.

The second story concerns the lovely River Alness. It was the last day of a frustrating week, and the rain had thundered down all night. There was a brown torrent going down the river, and I asked Bill Topham, the river superintendent, where he thought there might be some slack water. He directed me to the Douglas Fir Pool, where there was an angler worming on the opposite bank. I started with normal August flies, which would not stop skating on the surface, so I put on a Tweed tube of about 8 cm (3 in), with a brass body. On the end of the floating line, the only line I had with me on that holiday, this fly sank perhaps 30 cm (1 ft) below the chocolate-coloured surface. I caught three fish, all from the same lie, in the space of an hour. Staggering back to the car park with almost 18 kg (40 lb) of salmon on a lanyard over my shoulder, I met a party of other anglers who were drowning their sorrows with hip-flasks, and who all agreed that I had been wasting my time. There was a stunned silence then a flow of bad language when I flopped the three fish down beside the boot of my car. I told them how I had done it, and asked them if they had a sinking line. One of them had, so I told him where I had caught the fish, and where the lie was. I heard afterwards that he had caught two fish there, on a size-8 Stoat's Tail! I also heard afterwards that they had all quizzed the worm-fisher to see if I had snigged my fish, but having seen everything from a distance of 14 m (15 yd) he was able to assure them that all the hooks had been in the mouth!

Fishing is not a game measured by numbers, although many anglers think it is. They are delighted if they average more than one fish a day – some anglers are delighted if they average more than one fish a week. What they will never know is how many fish they might have caught if they had done something different. If they had been playing golf, or shooting at a target, they would have a mathematical score by which to judge their performance. Salmon fishing is like football. The team manager whose men have just won 2–0 will be reluctant to change a winning combination, even though he may have a niggle at the back of his mind that they should have won 4–0. There is no possibility of a replay with some variables built in. In salmon fishing, too, there is only a sense of success or failure, and all too frequently a nagging feeling that it might have been profitable to experiment. It may manifest itself in the car going home as the 'why didn't I try . . .?' syndrome.

Going back to the table of most-used flies in Scottish rivers, there is a sprinkling of both dark and bright flies, without any tendency for dark flies to be mentioned more often in the spring and autumn (when one might assume darker light conditions). Flies like the Willie Gunn and Garry Dog are mentioned just as often for March as they are for July. The Stoat's Tail is definitely a dark fly, yet it is frequently mentioned for July and August in the same breath as heatwaves and low water. When this idea first occurred to me several years ago, I was determined to reverse the rule and use bright flies in dull conditions, and vice versa, and I did not detect any reduction in my rate of catching salmon even when compared to anglers who stuck to the traditional rule.

So while I am not at all sure that the fly pattern makes the slightest difference to the fish, I am certain that it makes a great deal of difference to the angler. I *think* it makes a difference to the fish . . . and it is with that thought in mind that I write the rest of this book. If the pattern of fly does make a difference to the fish, and I am to trigger a feeding instinct when I offer my fly to a salmon, where should I start? Surely by looking at what the salmon were eating when they disappeared into the wild, blue yonder of the northern oceans.

4. WHAT DOES SALMON FOOD LOOK LIKE?

I must start by saying that, in writing this chapter, I have received unstinting help from several people. I have had my faith in human nature reinforced by picking up the telephone, asking a few questions, and receiving – by return – copies of scientific papers, photographs, references for further study, and even samples of stomach contents of salmon caught beyond the Faeroes.

I was once assured that, however abstruse a subject may be, there will be someone in the world who has made a study of it. I started with the Fisheries Laboratory at Lowestoft, where I spoke to Ted Potter. He provided me with copies of papers on the salmon's food while at sea in three locations. First, there was a paper by W. H. Lear discussing the food contents of salmon from the rivers of Newfoundland and Labrador. These fish migrate up along the coast of Greenland.

Next was a paper on the food of salmon in the Gulf of Bothnia, an arm of the Baltic where the salmon from the rivers of Finland and Sweden go to feed and grow. This paper was written by Jutila and Toivonen, of the Finnish Game and Fisheries Research Institute. Last, there was a paper by John Hislop and Alan Youngson of the Department of Agriculture and Fisheries for Scotland Marine Laboratories, Aberdeen. This is the one I could not put down until I had devoured it from end to end, as it referred to salmon from British rivers on their migration to the Arctic Ocean north of the Faeroes and roughly east of Iceland. The paper was written in 1983, and mentioned work that had been done in 1970 and 1971.

I must say here that I do not think I would be doing these men a favour if anything I said in this book encouraged every other angler to ring them up and ask for information. They are busy men, grafting away on various scientific projects, and in the present economic climate their time is precious, and measured out sparingly. I

27

hope, therefore, to pick enough detail out of the scientific papers to satisfy any normal angler and fly-tier, and thus avoid the need for anything other than further reading from the bibliography I list. If I do a good job on the mass of information before me, you won't need to look anywhere else!

Let us start with a generality, culled from the leading abstract of Lear's paper:

Examination of the contents of 2,350 stomachs from coastal areas and oceanic depths of the Northwest Atlantic Ocean suggests that Atlantic Salmon, *Salmo salar L.*, feed almost continually and fairly intensively while at sea and cease feeding as they approach the estuaries of their home river. Main items of diet were capelin, launce, herring, *Paralepsis coregonoides borealis*, amphipods, and euphausiids.

At that stage my eyes started to glaze over. What the hell was an amphipod? What did it look like? How did it move? What colour was it? I decided that further study was needed on all those Latin names.

I then turned to the paper by Jutila and Toivonen, motivated by the apparently huge mortality of salmon smolts in their first summer in the Baltic. It was found by these researchers that these little fish fed heavily on their way down the river on insects in their larval and nymph stages. On reaching the sea, they stayed in the top layer of water, nowhere more than 1 m (1 yd) deep, and that most of their food came from the top 30 cm (12 in) of water. As an average, 80 per cent of their food was insects (blown off the land) – midges, ants, and aphids. The remaining 20 per cent was made up of sticklebacks, although if the little salmon had swum deeper, into colder and saltier water layers a metre or so down, they could have had abundant food in the form of smelts. It was also found that salmon smolts did not start to switch from an insect diet to a fish diet until they had grown a few centimetres at sea, perhaps two or three months of growing. During this two- or three-month period the losses were very high, from a combination of starvation and being, in their turn, preyed upon – terns seem to be one of the main culprits.

Reading this paper, the thought crossed my mind that the little fish migrated to sea a couple of months before the supply of food there was ready for them, and I wondered if the migration is triggered by a rise in water temperature in the river. I then wondered if this temperature rise is due to de-forestation along the banks, allowing the sun to heat the river water more than it used to do before the forests were cut down! I cannot believe that nature planned these little smolts going to sea before their food supply was ready for them.

While this paper was fascinating, I felt it bore little relevance to the problems facing a fly-tier. I am not really concerned with the food of the salmon a year ago – what I want to know is the food it ate in such quantity a month or a fortnight ago, so that, when it sees my fly in the river it will recognise it as recent food.

I then turned to the paper by John Hislop and Alan Youngson, of the Aberdeen Laboratory, and I struck gold: here was a complete study of the food contents of the stomachs of salmon. Not only that, but also the salmon were most likely from British rivers, and they were large enough when sampled – a size range from the largest at 13 kg (29 lb) to the smallest, 3 kg (6½ lb). The sampling was done in March, and it is reasonable to suppose that some of the largest fish, if not most of the sample, would form part of the summer and autumn run into their home rivers.

Hislop and Youngson quote the results of previous research by Struthers, in 1970 and 1971, correlating this with their own results. The similarities are striking, although Struthers' area of sampling was further south, nearer to the Faeroes, and there was a higher proportion of fish in the later diet. All the samples of salmon from these three years – 1970 and 1971 by Struthers, and 1983 by Hislop and Youngson – were caught on a floating longline, in the upper 10 m (32 ft) of water. This suggests that adult salmon feed in the upper layers of the sea, and do not go down as deep as some people have suggested – I have heard it said that salmon feed so deep that there is almost no light penetration, and colours are no longer visible. I am sure that the Faeroese fishermen know a thing or two, and when they set their longlines at a maximum depth of 10 m (33 ft) they know exactly what they are doing, so I in turn can assume that salmon in the sea feed at such a shallow depth that they will be fully aware of the colours of their prey.

I am now going to get technical, and it will be safer for me to quote verbatim from the report by Hislop and Youngson. (This may save them from being bombarded with requests for copies, bless them!)

In 1983 the opportunity arose to examine the stomach contents of a further 48 salmon from Faeroese waters. These fish were a random selection of the commercial catch of the MV *Sundaenni*. They were caught by floating longlines, baited with sprats and set to fish in the upper 10 m of the water column. Although the 1983 samples were caught at a similar time of the year (late March) to those examined by Struthers they came from grounds considerably further to the north.

Forty-seven of the 48 stomachs in 1983 contained 'natural' food (the remaining stomach contained only bait). The percentages of occurrence of fish and crustacean prey were identical (92%). Fish made up the greatest part of the stomach contents of 30 of the salmon examined. The principal identifiable fish prey were lantern fishes (*Myctophidae*) which were found in 83% of the stomachs. Up to 28 individuals were recorded from a single stomach. Pearlsides (*Maurolicus muelleri*) were found in 12.5% of the stomachs but these rather small fish did not make a major contribution to the weight of the contents. Capelin (*Mallotus villosus*) were present in four stomachs and in three of these they were the dominant prey. A single specimen of barracudina (*Paralepsis* sp.) was found. Squid (*Todarodes* sp.) occurred in two stomachs and in one of these they were the main food item.

In 16 of the stomachs crustaceans constituted the greatest part of the food. The principal prey organisms were amphipods of the genera *Parathemisto* (including *P. libellula*, *P. Gaudichaudi* and *P. abyssorum*) and *Eusirus*. Although the former were generally smaller than the latter they were present in much larger numbers (frequently more than 500 individuals) and were the most important invertebrate prey. Euphausiids occurred quite frequently (in 44% of the stomachs) but they represented a relatively minor part of the weight of the stomach contents .... the importance of fish in the diet was much greater than had been observed by Struthers. Both studies

suggested that amphipods (*Parathemisto* spp.) are an important con-
stituent of the diet of salmon in Faeroese waters.

I read these golden words through, quite quickly the first time,
and then more slowly. I read them again and again, with a feeling of
bafflement growing in me. The Latin names were the key – if only I
could find out what these creatures looked like. It was at this stage
that John Hislop came up trumps. Not only did he point me to
further reading but he also actually sent me photographs and samples. As I sit here typing this, I have in front of me a little jar
containing perhaps half-a-dozen shrimp-like creatures that he tells
me are *Parathemisto* and euphausiids, and to take a photograph of
these creatures was merely a matter of time and a bit of fiddling with
trays of water. The photographs he sent were taken by a colleague of
his, Mr G. Howard, and they showed me what a squid called
Todarodes looks like – to my utter amazement the specimen photographed was 30 cm (1 ft) long! The thought flashed through my
mind of the sort of comment one would receive from a ghillie if one
attached a salmon fly of this size to the end of one's leader!

Going back to the report, there was a table showing the number
and total weight of food, species by species, salmon by salmon. It
was possible to work out the average weight of each food item, and I
did this for the salmon that had the squid as the main food item –
two squid weighing a total of 25.6 g each (about half an ounce).
They were hence considerably smaller than 30 cm (1 ft) long, but
they would be the same basic shape and, at a guess, perhaps 8 cm
(3 in) long.

At this stage I talked again to John Hislop. First, he assured me
that the colour of the samples of *Parathemisto* and euphausiids was
changed only slightly by the action of the digestive juices – they had
lost their apparent transparency a little. Second, he told me that I
was not necessarily correct when I assumed that salmon fed only in
the upper layers of the ocean. No work has been done on the depths
at which salmon feed, and while some of the creatures found in the
stomachs did live at considerable depths, they all tended to migrate
vertically, particularly at night. It was not possible to say whether
the salmon had eaten some of these creatures deep during the day,

or whether the salmon stayed shallow and only fed on these food-forms at night when they came near the surface. He then told me that daylight penetrates only to perhaps 9 or 12 m (30 or 40 ft) below the surface in clear water and that, in the North Sea, a diver who cuts him- or herself at a depth of more than 9 m (30 ft) will see their blood coloured black in the water. Whether a fish would see that blood as red or black at that same depth is a moot point.

Some of the shrimp-like creatures that live at great depths are coloured bright red, but because light does not penetrate to such depths they will appear black when they are down there. When they are near the surface, perhaps at dawn and dusk, they may appear somewhere between red and black. If you take a child's paintbox and mix red and black together, what do you end up with? Purple. And might that be a key to a puzzle – why on earth do salmon take a purple prawn? Because they see prawn-like creatures in the ocean, on which they feed avidly, and which at certain depths and at certain times of the day appear purple? Nobody knows for certain.

I am not aware of any research done into the depths at which salmon feed at different times of the twenty-four hours, but it is logical to assume that they will follow their food supply. The food migrates vertically, so may the salmon. So will all the other predators. But I think it is equally logical to assume that the salmon will see their prey in the same colours as we would, which is in its natural colours when near the surface and black when it is deeper.

It could also be logical to assume that the salmon stay near the surface and feed on the deep-living organisms only when these migrate upwards at night. Might it be plausible that the salmon that had empty stomachs had found the baited hooks late in the day, after they had digested the previous night's food? At present we cannot tell.

What is certain is that some members of the salmon family do feed at considerable depths. Off the west coast of Canada and the USA, where sport-fishing for species like coho takes place, it is not uncommon for the fish to be caught on rigs carrying sprats and other bait-fish at depths of 30 m (100 ft) or more. While it takes a lot of lead to take the bait deep like that, it is only just over 27 m (30 yd) after all, and is not the sort of depth we think of when we consider some of the ocean bottom and the creatures to be found there.

Table 2 Summary of research papers on the stomach contents of salmon from Faeroese waters.

	1970 2–18 April	1971 24 March–7 April	1983 28–29 March	Total
No. of stomachs examined	132	140	48	320
No. empty	48	50	0	98
No. containing food (incl. bait)	84	90	48	222
No. containing *vertebrates*	39	51	45	135
Sprattus sprattus (sprat)	32	38	12	82
Ammodytidae (sand-eel)	6	—	—	6
Clupea harengus (herring)	—	5	—	5
Maurolicus muelleri (pearlside)	—	3	6	9
Myctophidae (lantern fish)	—	1	40	41
Mallotus villosus (capelin)	—	2	4	6
Paralepsis	—	—	1	1
Unidentified fish remains	5	4	10	19
No. containing *invertebrates*	60	59	44	163
Todarodes sp. (squid)	—	—	2	2
Parathemisto spp. (shrimp)	[predominant]	57	40	157
Eusirus sp. (shrimp)	—	—	14	14
Euphausiids (prawn)	[few]	10	21	31
Calanus finmarchicus (copepod)	—	1	—	1
Other crustacea	—	—	9	9

Figures for 1970 and 1971 from Struthers, for 1983 from Hislop and Youngson.

Salmon are predators. All predatory fish tend to attack from below so that their prey is seen better against the light from the surface – silhouetted, black against light. The brighter the surface appears, the blacker will the prey appear, whatever colour it really is. Might this be a possible reason for black flies to be so successful? Then why should we have developed this old rule about the brighter the day, the brighter the fly? It does not seem logical to me, and in puzzling this out I can think of salmon caught that reversed the rule.

However, let us now look at the table of the research results of 1970, 1971, and 1983 to obtain a picture of the relative importance to the salmon of each of the food creatures (see Table 2.) We can then consider these creatures one by one to see what they look like, and to unravel these Latin names that are so baffling at first glance.

It should be noted that all these salmon were caught on longlines baited with sprats, and thus the figures for sprats in the stomach contents do not mean that these little fish would normally form as large a part of the diet as the figures in Table 2 suggest. But the salmon did eat them, or they would not have been caught. Of the twelve salmon containing sprats in 1983, all had only one, except for two that had two sprats, and one that had three sprats – but even these might have been taken off hooks further along the line.

VERTEBRATES

Vertebrates are animals with backbones. Fish have backbones, so all the creatures in the next few headings are fish of one kind or another. (See p. 102 for colour illustration.)

SPRATS

The main spawning area for sprats is in the south-eastern North Sea, and each female lays up to 10,000 eggs. The eggs hatch in about seven days, and the newly-hatched larvae are about 4 mm (¼ in) long. Sea currents carry the larvae along the coast of western Norway in a northerly direction, and when a year old they measure about 10 cm (4 in) in length. Their main food is animal plankton, particularly copepods. In Norway the one-year-old sprats have to be kept for three days so that the gut is emptied before they are preserved – either smoked, cooked, or in oil (brisling). The two- to four-year-old sprats are marinated and marketed as 'anchovies'.

Sexually mature at the age of two, when they are between 12 and 13 cm (4¾ and 5 in) long, sprats shoal in summer at depths of 10 to 50 m (11 to 55 yd), and in winter down to depths of 150 m (165 yd). By day the shoal stays deep, and at night the fish rise to the surface. The sprat is a silvery and greenish little fish. The 'Golden Sprat' of the bait-fishing salmon angler is dyed to this colour – the gold colour does not occur in natural sprats.

AMMODYTIDAE

Ammodytidae is the sand-eel to you and me. It is distributed all around the coast of the British Isles, and in a band from Orkney to Iceland, wherever there is a sandy bottom not at a great depth. Laid as a pile of eggs – up to 22,000 by one female – in small heaps on a sandy bottom, the larvae are 4 to 8 mm (⅙ to ⅓ in) long on hatching. The sand-eels feed on animal plankton, worms, crustaceans, and small fish and, north of Scotland, the spawning time is August to October, at which time the adults are from 15 to 20 cm (6 to 8 in) in length. Seldom found at depths greater than 30 m (33 yd), it frequently spends the day buried in the sand, but is active at night when it moves around in small shoals. A favourite food of salmon, cod, mackerel, and turbot, the sand-eel is unmistakable once seen – a long, skinny, silvery fish about 20 cm (8 in) long, which can move like greased lightning and disappear into the sand in an astonishing manner.

CLUPEA HARENGUS

The herring, in other words, and a favourite food fish of mackerel, salmon, haddock, and human beings. Soft bones and a high fat-content makes it a fish ideal for smoking into kippers, and when salted it will keep for a long time to become almost an essential part of the diet of northern European countries.

The main species of herring spawns along the coast of Norway, where a single female can produce 50,000 eggs. These are shed freely into the water, sink to the bottom, and hatch in about two weeks. The newly-hatched larvae – 7 to 9 mm (¼ to ⅜ in) long – are attracted to the light and rise to the surface. After a week they have consumed their reserve of yolk and start to feed on plankton. The scales form when they are about 4 cm (1½ in) long, and it is only when they are two to three years old and about 20 cm (8 in) long, that they move away from the coast. Becoming sexually mature at the age of between three and seven years, as soon as they have spawned they move north-west in search of food, reaching well north of Iceland. Estimated to live for a maximum of twenty to twenty-five years, they can reach a size of 40 cm (16 in). To give an idea of the numbers involved, the annual catch is reckoned to be between 2 and 3 million tonnes per year in the Atlantic and adjacent waters.

The herring has large scales, and looks silvery. When on the fishmonger's slab, the back appears greenish, but a shoal at sea can sometimes be detected as a violet patch in the water. Herring feed by sight, and thus mainly by day near the surface.

MAUROLICUS MUELLERI

Commonly called pearlsides, or sheppy argentine, this little fish has light organs along its underside. During the day it tends to go deep, down to 150 m (165 yd), but comes to the surface at night, where it is then found among the small herrings and sprats. Growing to a maximum length of 7 cm (2¾ in), it makes a handy mouthful for many predatory fish. In dim-light conditions, its flashing lights on the underside remind the observer of the silver ribbing on the bodies of many salmon flies!

MYCTOPHIDAE

This is known as the lantern fish. It is a small fish not unlike a minnow in shape and size, but it is coloured iridescent blue and silver, sheening to a mother-of-pearl. Dotted along the sides are luminous organs, which do not always shine. Lantern fish tend to migrate vertically, going deep during the day and coming to the surface at night. Looking at the figures in Table 2 of stomach contents, it will be seen that forty out of forty-eight salmon sampled had eaten lantern fish, and in another table, not reproduced, eighteen salmon had eaten more than ten lantern fish each – one had eaten as many as twenty-eight, weighing a total of 42 g (1½ oz). (This salmon was 6.8 kg – 15 lb – which gives one pause for thought when one considers a fish of this size eating little fish weighing 1.5 g – ½₀ oz – each, and about 5 cm – 2 in – long!)

Thinking about lantern fish, and flies to imitate them, how does one achieve luminous dots along the sides of a fly, and would they make any difference when fishing during the day?

MALLOTUS VILLOSUS

Capelin is the common name for these slim little fish that live almost entirely north of the Arctic Circle. At least that is what one book I have says they do, yet the survey by Hislop and Youngson was not as far north as that. Their survey showed that four salmon of the total of forty-eight had eaten capelin – one salmon had nine in its stomach weighing a total of 66 g (2⅓ oz), or an average of 7 g (¼ oz) each, so they must have been baby capelin.

Spawning at a temperature of 2–4°C (35–40°F), mating takes five seconds and up to 12,000 eggs are laid in a sand furrow at depths of 5–100 m (5½–110 yd). The eggs hatch in about four weeks into larvae about 4 mm (⅙ in) long. Becoming sexually mature at an age of two or four years, and at a size then of 13 to 20 cm (5 to 8 in), capelin migrate vertically, by day at depths of 150 m (165 yd), by night close to the surface – feeding on animal plankton. Capelin form an important part of the diet of cod, saithe, and whales. With their olive-green sheen on their silver sides, and prominent lateral line, capelin are unmistakable.

PARALEPIS

Called barracudinas, these little fish are so similar in shape to a sand-eel, but with a short dorsal fin, that they are not illustrated. Only one was found in the stomach of one salmon. They have prominent pointed teeth, large eyes, and are found normally in deep water over the continental shelf. The young fish tend to be found near the surface, but adults over perhaps 25 cm (10 in) are usually found deeper, and the absence of a swimbladder may well assist in this vertical migration. In more southern areas of the Atlantic, barracudinas are a favourite food of tunny.

That completes the descriptions of the fishes found in stomach contents by Struthers in 1970 and 1971, and by Hislop and Young-son in 1983. There can be no doubt that other fish are eaten by salmon if they get the chance – I cannot believe that a salmon, feeding avidly on everything that moves, is going to turn its nose up at any succulent mouthful that happens along. But the little fishes mentioned above form the bulk of available food – in that part of the ocean!

I think it is significant that there are only silvery fish in the list. There is nothing that would resemble a brown-and-gold Devon, or a Yellow Belly, for instance, and we can only assume that the salmon, when faced with one of these, will try to eat it, not because of its colour but because it is moving! Or is it possible that these little silvery fish in the sea will *appear* a different colour in certain conditions of light? Like a yellowy dawn or sunset casting a golden light under the surface? But then we think of those Devons, becoming more popular these days, coloured black and fluorescent orange, or brown and fluorescent yellow, and we take ourselves back to our mental drawing board!

INVERTEBRATES

We can now consider the invertebrates – those creatures without backbones. Except for the squid, all these creatures have the bones on the outside and the muscle in the middle, just as crabs and lobsters do. (And as do all the nymphs of our freshwater flies – one of the reasons why acid rain is so devastating to fly life, leaving, as it does, too little free calcium in the water for shell-forming.) (See p. 103 and p. 106 for colour illustrations.)

TODARODES

Most people call these squid. They can be any size from a few centimetres to a metre or so in length, and many species can change colour in less than a second. They can move forwards and back-wards – forwards by swimming and backwards by jetting water. The normal swimming speed is quite slow, but they can move at light-ning speed when propelled by that squirt of water – so fast that some species can jet-propel themselves out of the water and fly for many metres using their fins as planes for gliding. They are a favourite food of many fish, from tunny to mackerel and whales. The sample shown (pp. 98–100) is over 30 cm (1 ft) long, but those eaten by the salmon in the sample averaged about 14 g (½ oz) in weight, so they cannot have been more than a few centimetres in length. Normally a pale brown on top and creamy colour underneath, squid can change colour from white, through yellow to orange, red, purple, to almost black. With its eight sucker-bearing arms and two longer tentacles, it is an odd-looking creature, and looking at the illustra-tion I cannot help musing that the arms, if bent a little, could look just like the bends and points of an Esmond Drury treble!

PARATHEMISTO

Looking like a cross between a woodlouse and a freshwater shrimp (see p. 103) these little creatures were present in vast numbers in the sampling. One salmon had over 1,700 in its stomach, the total weight of which was only just over 28 g (1 oz)! One can only attempt to visualise the vast clouds of these little creatures swimming around in the sea, as seven of the salmon in the sample each contained over a thousand of these little shrimps.

Forming the staple diet for many sea creatures, from whales to fish, these little amphipods (creatures having two kinds of feet) tend to come up to the surface at night, and sink deeper during the day. Of a general sandy-fawn colour, with dark eyes, the samples I have been sent would be correctly imitated on a standard size 10 wet-fly trout hook. They have eight pairs of legs, the front five pairs being quite long, the rear three pairs noticeably shorter. There is a little flattened tail made up of a bunch of hair-like appendages. Looking at the samples, I am struck by the general buff colour, and have racked my brains for a salmon-fly recipe in that colour and cannot think of one – more food for thought?

EUSIRUS

Very similar to *Parathemisto*, *Eusirus* are larger, of a similar colour, but have little star-shaped blobs of colour on the back in a reddish tinge. About 25 mm (1 in) long, they do look very like a freshwater shrimp. Weighing approximately one third of a gram each, or about one hundred to an ounce, they would be correctly imitated on a single size 4 salmon-hook. Not nearly as numerous as *Parathemisto*, the maximum number in any one salmon's stomach was five.

EUPHAUSIIDS

These look like prawns, but the ones eaten by the salmon in the sample were pretty small – 0.14 gm average, or about two hundred to an ounce. Almost half the salmon had eaten these creatures, although the maximum number in any one stomach was six. If you imagine needing three hundred to make a reasonable prawn cocktail, you might get some idea of the size (assuming that, when we peel a prawn, we discard one-third of the total weight). At this size, most species of prawn are nearly transparent. There is the odd touch of colour, but on the whole they have a watery look to aid in their

39

camouflage. (There are deep-water species that tend to be coloured a deep reddish-orange, but these are found mainly in the great depths over the edge of the continental slope, and I might be so bold as to suggest that feeding salmon seldom see prawns of this colour.)

In common with much of the plankton, these prawns migrate upwards at night and go deeper during the day. For a creature about 25 mm (1 in) long, it is a remarkable achievement to be able to migrate upwards at a rate of 90 m (300 ft) an hour.

When swimming downwards, these creatures can achieve 128 m (420 ft) in an hour. There is one significant feature of all these little prawn-like creatures – they all have luminous red spots that at times they can flash with a brilliant light. These spots appear at the base of the second and seventh pair of front legs, and then there are four singles along the abdomen that shine vertically downwards, and one on the inside of each of the eye-stalks. Food for thought – what about a ribbing of fluorescent red floss on a prawn-shaped salmon fly that is an overall watery colour?

CALANUS FINMARCHICUS

There is no simple name for this little creature, other than to say it is a copepod. Looking at the sketch of this creature on p. 103 one realises that it is the size of a grain of rice, and that only one salmon was found with any in it. I think you will agree with me that it is not worth much investigation. Having said that, a grain of rice would fill a size 14 hook-shank, and the antennae when bent back could look like the bends of a double hook. The trouble is that the antennae bend back when the animal is travelling forwards, and a double hook would be travelling backwards when fished. These little cope-pods exist in the sea in countless millions, are the favourite food of herrings, and in the normal state are almost transparent. However, when they are invaded by a parasite called *Paradinium* they turn bright red, and this state can be as common as one in a hundred. A suggestion for a sea-trout fly?

This concludes our study of the creatures found inside salmon on their ocean feeding grounds. I have tried to keep it simple, and to concentrate on those aspects that could be of interest to the angler and fly-dresser. If there is food for thought for you, I shall be well pleased, not only while you are sitting at the fly-tying vice concocting something, but also while you are at the waterside trying to make your creation move as you imagine the real creature would be moving. And might I suggest that this movement will not be the smooth, steady progression across the pool so beloved of all the writers I have ever read on salmon fishing? Most of the creatures I have described tend to move slowly when not alarmed, but in short dashes if they sense danger. I have made a vow that I will try some short, sharp dashes with my fly in future!

This vertical migration is not confined to the sea. Every stillwater angler knows that algae migrate vertically, going deep in bright weather, and midge pupae, among other creatures, can migrate back to the bottom if conditions are too bright for their liking when they are near to hatching. Why, then, if fish know about this vertical migration, should we fish a fly near the surface in bright conditions, and deeper in dull cold conditions? If we are trying to imitate the natural food, should we not be doing opposite to what has become tradition? Is it not possible for the theory of greased-line fishing within a centimetre or so of the surface to be all wrong? Might we not catch more salmon by fishing near the surface in dull conditions, and using a fast-sinker in bright weather?

5. WHAT MATERIALS ARE USED IN A MODERN SALMON FLY?

An understanding of the materials available today may help fly-dressers to broaden their outlook when attempting to dress more life-like salmon flies. If you read this chapter, I must assume that you follow, and agree with, my premise that future development of the salmon fly should be aimed towards making the fly look more like the food the salmon ate in the sea. If you do not agree with me, you will presumably already have thrown the book aside as useless!

In the past, many exotic plumages were regarded as being essential for the proper dressing of a salmon fly. This belief, I can say with some certainty, is dead. A salmon fly can be tied using only a bunch or two of hair lashed on a hook, and it will catch fish. I propose, therefore, almost to ignore feathers – there are plenty of excellent books on salmon flies that go into the greatest detail, and I would merely be repeating old knowledge.

Having said that, I would not like to be without the following feathers in my fly-tying kit.

FEATHERS

TEAL FLANK-FEATHERS
There is no other material that can duplicate the effect of teal feathers, suggesting as they do the barring of a little fish. If you look at a baby mackerel you will see what I mean.

MALLARD BRONZE FEATHERS
I do not know why these feathers should be so useful, and why no substitute can be found, but they do make a brown version of the teal flank-feathers above, and the fish certainly like them. It can be no accident that these feathers are an essential part of the dressing of

42

such favourites as Blue Charm, Jeannie, and Thunder and Lightning, to name only three.

GOLDEN PHEASANT TIPPETS AND TOPPINGS

There can be few traditional salmon patterns that do not contain these feathers. The tippets have a nice, orange glow with black bars across, and the toppings have a golden, ethereal quality. They please human eyes, and seem to make a salmon fly more attractive. The tippets form most of the dressing of Colonel Esmond Drury's General Practitioner fly.

COCK HACKLES

Hackles for bearding can be made of hair, but hackles for palmering must be made of feather. If you like a palmered hackle, therefore, you need a supply of reasonably long cock hackles, dyed in an assortment of colours.

GUINEAFOWL HACKLES

Nice and cheap, these feathers can be dyed in various colours and give a good speckled effect on a fly. Ginger is one of my favourite colours.

Almost any other feather in common use on modern salmon flies can reasonably have hair substituted for it.

HAIR

Hair of value to the fly-dresser comes in many guises. The animal can be large or small, and the resulting hair can be stiff or soft. I have narrowed my own selection down to the following.

BUCKTAIL

Bucktail is the tail of the whitetail deer, but a useful substitute is the tail of a fallow deer from the UK. The hair is brown on top and white underneath, and one tail, when dyed, will give a range of shades from light to dark according to the part of the tail the hair comes from. The hair is reasonably stiff, but still moves in an attractive way when fished in faster currents. The hair on the underside of the tail is up to 13 cm (5 in) long, the dark hair on top of the tail perhaps half that length. Like all deer hair, bucktail hair is hollow, and tends to be slightly brittle.

SQUIRREL TAIL

The grey squirrel is an egg-eating pest, and is worth a cartridge whenever it is seen. The tail it provides is the animal's only benefit to humanity, although some people seem to get pleasure out of its antics on a birdtable – if they only realised how many more little birds they would have if every grey squirrel were shot!

The tail should be cut off as soon as possible after death, and well dried out in a warm place to mummify the meat before it putrifies. Done properly, you will have a tail with a stiff bone through the centre, into which the hairs are locked solid. If the hair can be pulled out in clumps, the tail was not dried properly. The tail can be used in its natural colour to give nice, barred hairs, or it can be dyed to a selection of colours. If dyed in its original state, the effect will be hairs that are coloured on the tips, but with darker bars on each hair. I would suggest that brown is one of the most useful colours, almost a chocolate colour, for use as a substitute for mallard bronze feathers.

The technique for bleaching squirrel tails before dyeing is now well known, and results in a solid colour on each hair, without the dark bars. If a selection of colours is obtained, these hairs can be used for winging and hackling, and I would not like to be without my collection of red, yellow, orange, blue, green, brown, black, grey, and ginger. A partly-bleached tail is an attractive buff colour. Whenever a piece of squirrel hair is cut off a tail, think of economy and save the discarded fluff from the base of the hairs to use as dubbing – it makes an excellent seal's fur substitute.

If you analyse the patterns shown in colour later in the book you will see that most of my salmon flies use squirrel-tail hair in one form or another – it is softer than bucktail, not as brittle, and if the tail is selected carefully, hairs of a great length can be found near the tip.

There is one fly for which the grey squirrel does not provide a good wing, and that is the Hairy Mary. The colour that seems to work best on the wing of this fly is a deep ginger colour, and while it is just possible to dye a bleached grey-squirrel tail this colour, the best hair comes from the tail of the fox squirrel.

One other useful squirrel tail comes from the parey squirrel, and can be used as a substitute for bronze mallard, as the colouring of barred dark brown, black, and grey gives a pleasing effect on a fly. Good squirrel tails can be obtained by mail order from Tom Saville and Steve Parton, to mention two of the tackle dealers with whom I am happy to trust my money.

DEER HAIR

The inclusion of deer hair might surprise some readers, but you will see the inclusion of the Muddler Minnow in the range of flies later in the book, and for this fly, good deer hair is essential.

I say good deer hair advisedly, as some of the rubbish sold to the unsuspecting will just not spin properly. The hair must be fine, dense, and not brittle. In the UK, this means just one kind of skin – that from the winter coat of a roe deer. As bucks are out of season in the winter, that means a roe doe. The hair from a red deer, or a fallow deer, is too coarse, and does not spin or pack well. If you can obtain a winter skin from a muntjack or Chinese water deer, this will do just as well as roe, but it must be a winter skin.

If you are lucky enough to have a deer-stalker friend, cadge a skin, spread it out on the garage floor, scrape as much of the meat and fat off it as will come off easily, and cover it with 25 mm (1 in) of alum powder. Leave it for a couple of weeks, then put the alum back into the jar for the next skin. Your skin will be hard and dry, ready to be cut up into convenient-sized pieces to sell to your fly-tying friends! Cut from the meat side, with a sharp knife, going through only the skin thickness, and you will not cut too much hair on the other side. Keep the tail end, with its lovely white rump hair, for yourself – this will be better than any bleached hair you can buy, and will dye to any colour you like if you degrease it thoroughly.

MAN-MADE MATERIALS

In the last few years, man-made materials have assumed great importance in fly-tying. The addition of glitter, sparkle, and flash has transformed some patterns. Later in the book you will see the use made of some of the materials mentioned.

Quite apart from the usual flat and oval tinsels in silver, gold, and colours like copper and green, which have been around for years, we now have flash and glitter in a bewildering array of colours.

FLASHABOU

This was perhaps the first of these glitzy materials, and Lureflash followed closely behind. I do not find that there is much to choose between them, but Flashabou is imported into the UK, and thus more expensive, than Lureflash. Both of them are multi-filament strands, very mobile and soft, with a glitter of many colours being available. Sometimes more than one colour flashes out of one bunch as, for example, in Lureflash mosaic or pearl. The addition of some of this modern material to the wing of a tube fly makes a great deal of difference to the eye-appeal of the fly – I hasten to add, to human eyes!

TWINKLE

This is a more recent version of these glittery fibres, and carries a tight twist that, when each fibre is moved, sends out a shower of points of light. Again, most attractive to human eyes, and probably also to the fish!

MYLAR TUBING

Available for some years from Veniards in silver and gold, there is now a pearl version of Mylar tubing available that makes a fantastic tube-fly body, reflecting the colours of the wing, and showing through whatever underbody is applied. For the effect of this mate-rial, see some of the tube flies illustrated later. I can think of no better material to give the effect of the scales of a small fish.

ARTIFICIAL HAIR

Ever ready to make a quick buck, our American friends have devised all sorts of substitutes for hair. A popular material on that side of the

Atlantic is polar-bear hair and as these animals are protected, the supply of hair from them is almost non-existent. A fine, nylon hair was developed, originally I think for doll's hair, and is sold under the name Fishair. Dyed in a great range of colours, I have used it only a few times and found it to clog a bit when wet, but some people swear by it for a fine, mobile hair effect when used as wing. I prefer to mix Fishair with other hairs like bucktail to reinforce the wing slightly, and when used in this way it does add a sparkle not obtainable with hair alone. You can obtain a similar effect by colouring 900 g (2 lb) nylon with a felt pen, coiling it around the fingers, cutting through the coils, and thus obtaining lengths about 10 cm (4 in) long for use in winging. In the early days of this century, Baden-Powell invented a series of flies using lengths of gut dyed in various colours for the wings, and called these Prismatic flies – they had a translucence and sparkle that was thought to be attractive to salmon – but the gut was not left straight, it was deliberately put into curls by being drawn between finger and thumb-nail.

There are many other man-made materials available to fly-dressers if they keep their eyes and minds open. Christmas decorations supply unlimited tinsel effects. Plastic carrier-bags are printed in a variety of colours and can be cut into strips for winding around hooks, or into shapes for the carapace of shrimp or prawn patterns. Fertiliser sacks are thicker than shopping bags, and perhaps better for this latter purpose. Spirit felt-pens give a waterproof ink that will stick to plastic, and can be used to colour or add a pattern to shapes you cut out. The field is almost limitless, and if you are constantly alert to the possibilities around you, it need cost you nothing. To give but one example, I went to a conference many years ago in a hotel that had recently had a new carpet fitted in the conference hall. I spent two mind-boggling days of utter boredom shuffling my feet, and at the end I had the consolation of a pocketful of beautiful olive-dun-coloured dubbing material from that carpet. There is still a little plastic bag of it in my fly-tying kit, and I have tied many dozens of nymphs with it over the years.

Many years ago, Tom Saville used to sell the hair from the silver baboon. This was barred black and white, and made an ideal substitute for teal. It is unobtainable nowadays, to my great regret, and many fly-dressers have difficulty mounting neat wings with teal feathers. A fortune awaits the person who can produce a hair, or a substitute hair, barred like a teal feather as the fish-appeal of this particular item is undoubted.

What materials can be used for a modern salmon fly? Anything at all, providing it yields the effect you are seeking, and the fish like it. But first it has to please you, or the fish do not have the opportunity of giving their verdict.

6. WHAT DO I DRESS A SALMON FLY ON?

If one goes back about one hundred and fifty years to the 'golden age' of salmon fishing, we find salmon flies of the traditional type evolving from what were really enlarged trout flies. Once these so-called traditional flies had been developed, they were not to change in their basics for nearly a hundred years. The first mention of an eyed hook is to be found in O'Gorman's *Practice of Angling*, published in 1845, where the author shows very plainly his dislike of the 'newly-invented hook ... with an eye in the shank. It is another Scotch invention, and as to its usefulness it may be placed on a par with the newly-invented method of breeding salmon. Any fly tied on a hook of this description must be clumsy'.

In the second edition of Stoddart's *Angler's Companion* of 1853, there is mention of an improvement in the salmon fly of recent date, namely 'the substitution, as a mode of attaching it to the line, of a small loop or eyehole of gut at the head or shank-end of the hook, instead of a full length of the same material'. It is tempting to suppose that this is the 'Scotch invention' so scorned by O'Gorman. The eyed trout fly hook of H. S. Hall came on the market much later, about 1875.

The gut loop-eye was being praised for its ability to impose less strain on the cast by virtue of its having an elastic joint between metal and cast as recently as the mid-1930s! Certainly in 1919, with the publication of Chaytor's *Letters to a Salmon Fisher's Sons*, it was suggested that a violin E-string formed durable and pliant loops for gut eyes.

It was Pennell who first suggested returning the wire to form a loop-eye, rather than the circular ring-shaped eye. Cheap hooks with a ring-eye sometimes had a gap between the shank and the end of the metal that could cause fraying of the cast. Early, cheap loop-eyes did not have the metal thinned first, and were clumsy at the point where the wings of the fly were tied on. Cholmondeley-Pennell's first

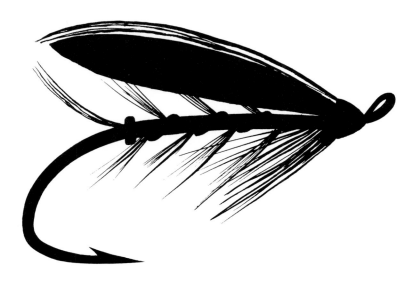

This is the silhouette of a traditional salmon fly, tied on a large, single hook for over one hundred years, with originally a gut loop for the eye, or direct to the gut leader. The loop-eye, with the leg of the loop tied down under the head, was thought to be stronger than a ring-eye.

Fly-dressing as an art-form demands that the fly should be 'balanced', and for this human conclusion the butt and root of the tail had to be directly over the barb, and the tail and topping had to meet in a point no further back than the bend of the hook. The throat hackle had to emanate from the same place as the wing, and if the wing was made up of many different materials, these had to be married together so that the wing looked one solid piece.

If you half-close your eyes and look at this silhouette, could it be possible for a salmon to see that solid wing as the body of a shrimp, with everything else representing legs, bunches of eggs, tail, and feelers? It is even easier to visualise this if the wing is laid slightly flatter along the body of the hook.

attempt at a metal eye involved brazing a separate piece of metal to the shank, and was invented about 1873. It seems incredible that gut loop-eyes were still popular over fifty years later, particularly for large flies.

So much for hooks. What about the flies tied on them? If we look at a typical salmon fly of the 1850s, it will be fully dressed. With a tag, butt, tail, body in perhaps several sections, all with butts or veiling between, palmered hackles, head hackles, and a wing consisting of perhaps ten different strands of feather married together, with cheeks, horns, and toppings, it was a resplendent example of slave labour and the demise of many exotic fowl.

Today there are some fly-dressers who delight in being able to reproduce these old patterns, and as an art form in itself it gives great pleasure to the artist and the onlooker alike. The rare feathers are impossible to obtain nowadays – many of them are illegal even to possess – and luckily for the salmon angler of today, these flies are totally unnecessary.

One of my prized possessions is an Alexander Martin catalogue of 1937, and fully-dressed salmon flies were being offered at prices

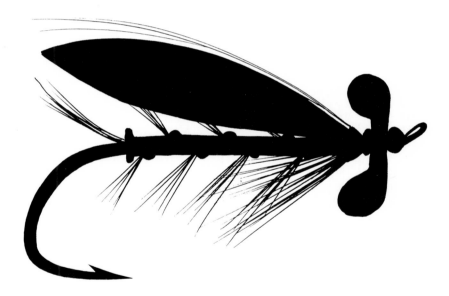

A variation of the traditional salmon fly, sold by Hardy's many years ago as the Aaro Spinner. The intention was to add a spinning blade in front of a traditional salmon fly to give extra flash. I have been told that a court case resulted from the use of this fly in 'fly-only time' on the Tweed, but I am not certain of the truth of this. The ball-shape either side of the spinning blade was made of metal, and the fly had a normally-finished head behind the rear, metal ball.

51

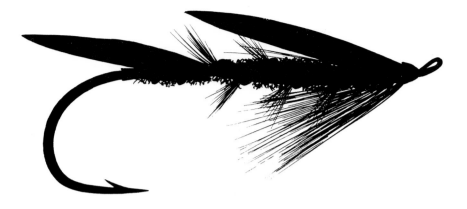

The 'Four-in-Hand' fly, evolved on the Stinchar and on the Tay. Tied on longshanked hooks, this style with four wings set in two pairs was needed, it was thought, because of the lack of a feather with a web long enough to span the length of the shank. The result is a slim dressing, which swims smoothly through the water, but what it represents can be anyone's guess. Seldom seen nowadays, this style goes back into the later part of the last century.

ranging from 2/3d (11p) for a size 2, up to 3/6d (17½p) for a size 6/0. Names like Jock Scott, Thunder and Lightning and Durham Ranger, Dusty Miller, and Silver Wilkinson conjure up magic pictures for me, of patterns that had then lasted for a hundred years, and that are still going strong fifty years later, although the flies tied under those names today may well be simplified almost to the point of being unrecognisable.

To put these prices in context, an old friend of mine joined the army in 1938 and his pay as a recruit was 7/6d (37½p) per week. He did not draw all of that, of course, as there was a deduction for barrack damages, clothing, and other items, so that he drew about 5/- (25p) per week. If you think that two fully-dressed salmon flies cost a private's pay, it might give you some idea that salmon fishing in those days was the hobby of the rich, and you would be right.

Low-water flies developed largely as a result of the writings of A. H. E. Wood, in the 1920s – basically a slightly longer shank, lighter wire, and a fly dressed only on the front part of the shank. Wood fished the Dee at Cairnton at a time when the river was producing incredible numbers of fish, and he was able to experiment – he even tried single hooks on which there was no dressing whatever, and he caught fish. He did have one problem. He found himself losing a lot of fish after they had been hooked and, surprisingly for the chairman of BSA with lots of engineering brains available to him, his conclusions proved entirely wrong. He tried to solve the problem by lengthening the shank of the hook, ending up by using hooks that today would be described as 6X long. He still lost a lot of fish. If he had tried offsetting the point of his single hooks, he would have lost far fewer. Even today, I cannot think of a hook manufacturer who offers single salmon hooks with an offset point – or in any colour except black, or with any eye except a loop up-eye!

The low-water style of salmon fly, created because of a desire to use a smaller fly without the need to lose the hooking power of a large hook. This style is also seen on double hooks even today, and traditional patterns can be abbreviated and simplified to fit the smaller space available when using only half the shank length for the dressing.

What does the salmon think about that great chunk of ironmongery sticking out behind the small fly? Not much, apparently, or the style would not be as well-used, nor as successful, as it is. There does, however, seem a slow decline in the popularity of this method of tying, say, a size-8 fly on a size-4 hook. Today, most anglers would choose to use a size-8 treble with a size-8 fly dressed on it, and have more reliable hooking power than any size of single hook.

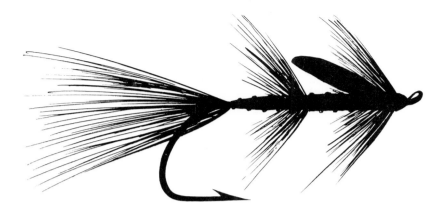

The traditional shrimp-style of dressing. The two parts of the body can be of different colours, and the hackles are usually also of different colours. Wings are not usually added, but a jungle-cock eye on each side of the head hackle, as in the example above, is common. This style can be dressed on singles, doubles, or longshank trebles, and is as popular today as it ever was, particularly in Ireland.

If you disbelieve me when I stress that offset points should be used for more reliable hooking, consider that a salmon (or a human being for that matter) has to press the tongue against the roof of the mouth while swallowing. Thus any object to be swallowed is automatically laid flat on the tongue, and so a salmon fly dressed on a single hook will be laid flat on its side at the very moment the line is tightening. There is a reasonable chance of a hookhold in the scissors if the gape is nearest to the throat, but it is a recipe for disaster if the gape is nearest to the nose of the fish. However, if the point of the hook is well offset, the point will almost screw itself into a good grip as soon as it meets any resistance. Whichever way the hook is lying, left side up or right side up, the point will still screw itself in to a good hookhold.

To test this theory, take two single salmon hooks: one with a straight point, and one which you have offset with a pair of pliers. Tie 1 m (1 yd) of nylon to the eye of each hook. Take a small piece of carpet offcut, or bacon rind, and fold it double. Pinch both hooks in turn between the folded material, and pull on the nylon. The flat hook will be found to pull out, without gripping, quite frequently. The offset hook will be found to grip nearly every time. You will have to carry out this experiment only once to be totally convinced. You will then go to get your flybox and gently offset the point of every single hook with a pair of flat-nosed pliers. And from then on, you will lose far fewer fish.

Before I get involved in much correspondence, may I say that it does not matter in the least whether the hook is kirbed or reversed, or offset to left or right. One way will grip in the roof of the mouth, and the other way will grip in the tongue, but this will then be reversed when you fish off the opposite bank, and it would be pure semantics to become involved in arguments in favour of one or the other. As long as the point is offset, it matters not in the slightest which way it sticks out.

Double hooks seem to me to be half-way between extremes. They do not have quite the reliability of hooking enjoyed by the treble, nor the screwing-in ability of the offset single, and I tend not to use them at all nowadays. I am not sure when they were first invented, but they look nice when a fly is dressed on them. They give a balanced

The Waddington shank, using a steel shank and a small treble hook attached. The dressing can look very sleek and slim when moving through the water, even on early patterns that used feather wings and long heron hackles. Nowadays, hair has replaced the feather fibre used, and the flies can look just as sleek providing not too much hair is used in the dressing. Early patterns had a butt and tag added to the treble, but these are seldom seen nowadays. It is usual to lash a piece of nylon monofil to both the shank and the treble, to keep the hook in line with the body.

The tube fly, shown here on a heavy brass tube with a rubber sleeve for the eye of the treble. Tubes can be of any length and thickness, from slim, plastic tubes to those of brass almost 6 mm (¼ in) in diameter. Those made of metal with a plastic covering on the outside (Supatubes) avoid the need for the rubber tubing, as they have a built-in recess for the eye of the treble.

Nowadays, most spring and autumn fishing in our larger rivers is done with tube flies of one kind or another. By using combinations of different sinking lines, lengths of leader, and weight of tube fly, the water can be searched at whatever depth one chooses. Special treble hooks are available with slim, oval eyes that fit more easily into the rear of a tube fly, commonly called needle-eye trebles. The eye is not the same as that on a needle but is just a slim, narrowed version of a round eye.

appearance to a fly, sink slightly more quickly than a single, and are favoured by many salmon anglers. Yet quite a few fish are lost after being hooked on a double hook.

The cure for these losses, to a considerable extent, would be for doubles to have offset points, with both points turned slightly outwards. Then they would screw themselves into a hookhold in the same way as the offset single does. Yet I do not know any hook-maker who makes double salmon hooks with out-turned points.

Tending to be forgotten nowadays is the fact that a man called John Parker started the use of treble hooks for salmon fishing. His Parker tube flies, invented around the same time as Waddington wrote his book in 1947, did not look as attractive to human eyes as did the Waddington shanks, and so never became popular. Parker used starling wing-quills, and other bird quills, to form tubes on which to dress flies, and used a mount of wire running through the quill with a treble on the end, rather like a Devon Minnow mount. He suggested winding lead wire around the mount for extra weight for spring and autumn fishing. His Parker Major tube flies used long hair-wings and looked shaggy and – to anglers in those days – nasty, and never caught the public's imagination.

Waddington's flies, tied and sold commercially by Alexander Martin, looked sleek and neat, and were a commercial success. Waddington originally called them Elverine lures, and they used feather in the dressing – I have not seen an original Waddington Elverine dressed with hair. For really long fibres, heron hackles seem to have been used. British Patent no. 10,246 covered these flies.

While the Waddingtons looked sleek and fishy even in the larger sizes, it is my personal impression that the treble hooks used were too small, and the rigid shank allowed a salmon to lever out the hold of the hook. Losses while playing salmon on Waddingtons tend to be fairly frequent, and I have heard similar comments about Toby spinners, perhaps for the same reason (see the picture of the Akroyd in the colour illustrations).

Made of hardened steel – the same hardened steel as hooks themselves – Waddington shanks are still available today, made by Partridge of Redditch. Available in single- and double-shanked versions,

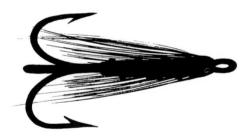

An early example of Esmond Drury's style. The whole of the dressing is within the total length of the hook, and the dressing is slim and streamlined. Normally the wing colour is tied in first, and then the hackle material is added on top of the wing, but is shorter. Early patterns had the hair distributed evenly around the shank as, despite the up-turned eye, it could not be certain which side of the fly would be uppermost when swimming through the water.

Early Esmond Drury flies had feather wings if the pattern specified these, and materials such as teal and mallard bronze were tied in small bunches. Later versions of Drury flies tend to use hair instead of feather.

Following the more modern trend for longer hair in flies, more recent Esmond Drury patterns are dressed longer. Early thoughts of the possibility of the hair wrapping itself around the hook bends proved groundless, and nowadays the hook can be almost buried in the roots of the wings. Longer, more mobile tails, and flowing wings well past the bends of the hooks are all signs of the more-modern Drury patterns.

the latter being slightly heavier, they have a loop-eye at one end and a ring-eye at the tail. By the time a good-quality treble hook has been attached to the ring-eye, they tend to be expensive, and I make my own out of paperclips. This is easily done by straightening out a large paperclip, bending the wire round a fine nail with a pair of pliers to form a neat eye at each end, and making sure that there is sufficient wire left in the middle to form an overlap. With a good whipping of sewing-thread along the shank to hold the overlap together (*after* hooking the treble in), these have never let me down in fishing. Starting with such cheap, raw material, it is not a cause for tears when the dressing wears out and a pair of wire cutters is used to recover the treble hook.

Waddington shanks allow the treble to flop around too much for my taste, and I always lash a piece of nylon along the shank of the treble and under the dressing to stiffen the hinge a little (2.75 kg – 6 lb – nylon is stiff enough for this purpose). When sold by Alexander Martin in the 1950s and 1960s, these flies always had a dressing put on the treble hook as well as on the shank – usually a floss tag and a butt of ostrich herl – and this seemed to make a neat, attractive finish to the fly. Today, few anglers bother with this dressing on the treble.

The big disadvantage of the Waddington shank is that the fly stays attached to the treble hook, and this sometimes seems to give the fish the ability to lever out the hook during play. A tube, on the other hand, will slide up the leader, out of the way, leaving the treble firmly stuck into the fish. I do find that I lose fewer fish on tubes than I do on Waddingtons and, for this reason alone, I seldom nowadays use anything but tubes when I want a long salmon fly.

Tubes are available in a variety of weights. The lightest are made of plastic – not, I would hasten to add, the hard, nylon tubing mentioned so often in the tackle catalogues, but PVC or polythene tubing. This is the only material that will bell out at the ends when heated – nylon does not do this, but merely burns or scorches.

A free source of tubing is the empty ball-point pen, discarded in huge quantities in any large office. Cut to length, offered to a smoke-free flame, the end will bell out nicely to keep the dressing in place. If you use a candle for this, you will end up with black fingers and messy tubes. A ring on the gas-cooker, or a small butane blowlamp, will leave you with clean fingers and tidy tubes.

Slightly heavier are aluminium tubes, with a plastic lining either inside or outside. Again, these can be bought in any length, and the flies dressed on them can be regarded as slow-sinkers, whatever length they are. It is a mistake to use a longer tube to get a higher rate of sink – it is better to use a heavier tube of the length you decided was correct for the water being fished.

Heavier still are brass tubes, and these can be made of fine-bore or heavy brass. Again, they will probably have a plastic lining either inside or outside the tube, and can be of any length. An 8-cm (3-in) brass tube will sink like a brick, and is a fearsome thing to cast. If it catches you behind the ear on a forward cast, you will feel as if Mohammed Ali belted you one, and the key to casting these large tubes is to shorten the leader down to a maximum of 1.25 m (4 ft). It is a recipe for disaster to use a heavy tube on the end of 4.5 m (15 ft) of 4.5 kg (10 lb) nylon.

The tubes with the plastic on the outside of the metal are nowadays hard to find, but I find them most convenient to use as they have the socket at the tail for the treble hook already built in, and the fly does not need a separate piece of tubing to hold the hook. Since bicycle tyres were redesigned some years ago, the easy source of rubber valve tubing has dried up. When dressing these Supa-tubes, as they are called, one should take the dressing only as far as the end of the metal, leaving the plastic part naked. Thus the dressing is fully supported by the metal liner.

When comparing tubes with Waddingtons, there is one further benefit of the tube that must be mentioned. If you decide that your fly is too small, you can add another tube to the leader, or even two further tubes. Three 25-mm (1-in) tubes will give the effect of one 8-cm (3-in) tube, and this versatility is impossible with Wadding-tons. It is also possible to ring the changes on colour – an assortment of bright and dark tubes can be juggled to give a fly with a dark head and bright tail, for instance.

For many anglers, the hooking ability of tubes and Waddingtons give cause for concern. I have heard people say that if one lands 50 per cent of the fish hooked, one is about average. This blind accept-ance of the poor hookhold when salmon fishing has filled page after page of fishing books and magazine articles, usually concentrating on the old argument, to strike or not to strike. It has occurred to me that many of the lost fish were lost on tubes or Waddingtons, and looking at some of the tackle used by my fellow salmon anglers leads me to wonder whether, the treble hooks were big enough to yield a good hold in the first place. Nowadays I use quite large treble hooks on my tubes, and I think I have lost fewer fish.

I recall a day on the Tweed some years ago, when I lost the first four fish of the day, all in the space of an hour. In desperation I turned to the boatman, the late Willie Lee, and asked him what I was doing wrong. With a cheery grin, he said, 'Nothing. Don't worry, the next one will stay on, and it will be bigger.' It did stay on, and it was even bigger, but I still think of that morning and what I could have done to prevent those fish coming off. Could I have used a larger treble on the tube fly? Could I have used a smaller tube fly with a smaller treble? Might the fish have taken a more confident hold if I had used finer nylon? We can never tell.

I must now stress that many of the flies shown in the colour illustrations are dressed on single hooks for one reason only: the dressing shows more clearly, and they lie flat nicely for photography. Nowadays I do not use single hooks for my salmon flies.

Chronologically we now come to the Esmond Drury treble hook.

Invented by Lieutenant Colonel Esmond Drury MC, these treble hooks have removed much of the aggro from salmon fishing. They hook fish with almost total reliability. I have lost only one salmon on a Drury treble, and I was so astonished that I still remember the sense of almost outrage I felt that it should have happened. I think I know why I lost that fish. It took me the instant the fly landed, and I got such a surprise at the huge slosh that I struck instantly, just like an idiot beginner. If I had counted two . . . three, and lifted the rod to feel for the fish, I am quite convinced that I would have protected the 100 per cent record Drury trebles enjoy with me.

Invented in the early 1960s, covered by British Patent no. 1,013,480 of 1964, these hooks have been copied by others since the patent ran out in 1980. It is my firm conviction that the copies are not quite as good at hooking as are the original genuine Drury trebles. Every copy I have ever seen has missed one small but essential feature of the Drury design. The design of salmon flies took a sudden change with the launch of Esmond Drury's hooks, and anglers in the future will have much to thank Esmond Drury for.

This brings us up to date on the shape of salmon fly hooks. What about the colour of hooks? When we go back far enough into the history of hook-making, we find that hooks were blued. As part of the hardening and tempering process, hooks were heated and dumped in oil, and the result was a blue finish not unlike a shotgun barrel. This was not sufficiently rust-resistant, so someone had the bright idea to lacquer hooks. Black japanning was a popular and common lacquer in use at the time, and thus black japanning came to be the accepted finish for salmon hooks – by sheer accident, I am sure. Today it has become entrenched in tradition, and salmon flies are impossible to sell commercially on bronzed hooks.

A fly-dresser sitting down to busk up some salmon flies reaches for a black hook. If that same person was going to dress some double-hooked flies for Loch Leven, even though they were the same size, he would reach for a bronze hook. Salmon flies do not look right unless they are on black hooks. Trout flies do not look right unless they are on bronze hooks. Is there a logical reason for this? I cannot think of one. It looks right. In other words, it looks the same as it always has, and reason has nothing to do with it!

Before the war, the same firm of Alexander Martin (whose win-

61

dow in Exchange Square, Glasgow, cost me ten minutes every day on my way home from school) sold hooks that were silvered. They claimed that the silver plating made the hooks invisible in water, as they reflected the colours around them. They were offered in every size from 3/0 to 15, and flies dressed on their Silverhooks were available at 2/- (10p) per dozen extra! More recently, Drury trebles are available in a nickel-plated finish in a restricted range of sizes, and articles have been written in the fishing magazines extolling the virtues of tiny Stoat's Tail flies dressed on silver-coloured trebles down to size 14 for summer salmon in dead low-water. Some examples of these tiny trebles are shown in the colour illustrations.

Red hooks are sometimes seen, usually on prawn and shrimp dressings, presumably with the idea that the hooks will blend in among feelers and tails and not be noticed by the fish. Bob Church is even selling green hooks to trout anglers, saying that the green hook is less visible under water. I cannot see this idea catching on with salmon anglers, who tend to be paranoic about the slightest piece of weed on the fly, and who will regard a green hook as being too similar to a piece of weed. But I must say I have heard very favourable comments from a few stillwater anglers about green hooks used in conjunction with a pheasant-tail nymph-dressing.

One thing that always makes me grin: I see lots of silvery spinning lures in shops, and a surprising number have silver-coloured treble hooks at the tail. Yet every little fish I have ever seen has a brown, fawn, or chestnut-coloured tail, so why not a bronzed treble at the tail of a spinner? More tradition?

A final credit must go to Esmond Drury for being the person who first decided to drop odd sizes of hooks, on the basis that a fish that had refused a size 8 was not likely to take a size 9. He then found that the rest of the hook-making industry was only too pleased to follow his example, and so today we can buy only even-numbered hook sizes.

The choice of base for a salmon fly is, therefore, wide. Hooks can be single, double, treble, normal shank or long-shank, light wire, standard wire, or heavy wire. Tubes can be of any length, of light or heavy material. Waddington shanks can be of any length, and you can add lead to the shank if you wish. What to choose? Let us start by supposing that you want a short, fat, hairy fly. Dress this on a hook. If you want a long, thin fly, dress this on a tube or Waddington. In other words, flies dressed on hooks will have a bulkier shape than if you dressed the same pattern on a tube. So the overall shape you require will determine the base for the fly. Shrimps, prawns, or squid are bulkier than little fish, so should perhaps be dressed on hooks. Little fish, on the other hand, are slimmer, and should be dressed on tubes or Waddingtons.

I can hear you telling me that your favourite fly is a Teal, Blue and Silver, that it represents a little fish, and that you always dress it on a double hook – so be it. I would still suggest that imitations of fish look better to my eyes if they are dressed slimly, and that this is best done on a tube or shank. The treble at the tail can represent the tail of the little fish. We could argue all day and we would both be right – or both be wrong. It matters not one jot providing each of us has a rationale for our own belief, and fishes with confidence and concentration as a result.

To summarise, therefore, the base for my chosen fly. From personal choice I pick up a tube for a slim fly, and an Esmond Drury treble for a bulkier-looking fly. But if you are a thinking fly-dresser you can tie fat flies on tubes, or thin flies on trebles! It is all a matter of personal choice. The choice must give you confidence. If it doesn't, the result of your efforts will sit in the flybox for years and never be used at all. And the fish cannot give their verdict if the fly never gets into the water!

7. WHEN IS A FLY NOT A FLY?

The question that the title of this chapter poses causes more argument, more anger, more heartburn, and more sullying of reputations in salmon circles, than almost any other I can think of. It assumes most importance on rivers where there is a 'fly-only' rule, either dictated by the calendar or by the height of the water. On Tweed, for instance, there is a period at each end of the fishing season when there are no nets in the lower reaches of the river, and while the nets are off, there is a fly-only rule applied to the whole of the river. Once the netting starts, this rule is relaxed, and one may spin, worm, or fish fly to one's heart's content. Now that netting rights have been bought by a conservation trust, which is devoted to maximise the runs of salmon into the river, it remains to be seen whether the fly-only rule will be applied in the future.

On many other rivers there is an agreement among the riparian owners that fly-only will be the rule if the water level is below a certain agreed height, and one sees anglers and ghillies making a study of the water level each morning to see what method may be used. It is for this reason that the gauge is usually on the river bank directly across from the fishing hut, where it can clearly be seen by all concerned immediately on arrival in the morning.

In the United States and Canada there is a slightly different rule – there it is called fly-rodding, and providing one is using a fly rod, fly reel, and fly line, there is less rigidity about what is tied on the end of the leader. Not everywhere is this rule applied – in some prestige rivers, the fly-only rule applies just as keenly as it does in many places in the UK. In addition to this, of course, in most places in North America, treble hooks are illegal, so Esmond Drury trebles would not be permitted. In some places the possession of a treble hook is illegal, and one is as guilty if a treble-hooked fly is reposing in the corner of a flybox as one would be actually fishing with it. I have heard that doubles are frowned upon in some places, and anglers using tube flies thus have to put a single hook behind the tube.

I do most fervently hope that nothing I say in this book will encourage anglers to break any rules. The rules of a fishery are something one is expected to accept with good grace. The people who drafted the rules did so for a purpose, usually to ensure that sport for everyone is as pleasant as possible, and to prevent the occasional bad sportsperson from spoiling fishing for others, or from catching more than their fair share, and fishmongering the results.

Yet there will be a growing problem in the future about whether something created at the fly-tying vice is, or is not, a fly. I talked to a highly-respected riparian owner of one of the more famous salmon beats recently and he told me that, in his view, a fly had to contain feathers, fur, or other natural materials in order to be classified as a fly. I then asked him if he could kindly investigate the rules for me – was there a definition laid down in writing? He checked for me and told me that there was not. He thought that most anglers could look at something and decide for themselves whether it could reasonably be described as a fly. So could his boatman. If anglers were asked not to fish with some creation, then that was that. If they persisted, and asked to be shown the rule book, the verdict would be to tell them to have fun, but they wouldn't be coming back next year. The ultimate sanction!

However, to insist upon only natural materials would make illegal perhaps the majority of salmon flies exposed for sale in the UK at the present time. Nylon threads, tinsels made of a plastic base upon which metal has been deposited, man-made fibre substitutes for seal's fur, artificial hair, pieces of latex used for the carapace of a prawn fly – all these fall outside the definition of 'natural materials'.

To go further, I have several tube flies in my boxes that contain no natural materials at all. They are dressed on brass-lined plastic tubes, using nylon thread, pearl Mylar tubing, and have wings of Lureflash. They *look* like tube flies. I have fished with them on the Tweed – indeed a Tweed boatman actually selected one of them from the box one difficult day – and I did not feel at the time that I was doing anything wrong. I confess that it never entered my head that I was breaking any rule, and would have been thunderstruck if I had been so accused!

Later in this book, I show illustrations of many flies that contain artificial or man-made materials. I must say straight away that to tie a Muppet onto an Esmond Drury treble does not make a fly – of that I am utterly certain. But there will be many borderline cases where, if you decide to have a go and make some, I would urge you to clear the pattern with your host or riparian owner before fishing with them. If you ask a ghillie and get a reply such as 'Well, it's OK with me, but don't let the boss see you', then don't use them. You will have received an answer that makes it clear that the ghillie thinks that they are not acceptable, but didn't want to offend you by telling you directly.

Later in the book, however, you *will* see a Muppet tied on an Esmond Drury treble. This book is entitled *Successful Modern Salmon Flies*. How can I reconcile this contradiction? Quite simply by catering for the time when you are fishing a river on which there are no rules about what constitutes a fly. The angler in the next pool may be spinning with a Devon or a Toby. You have a fly rod in your hand, and I see no reason why you should not use a Muppet on the end of your leader if you wish to. In these circumstances you are not breaking any rule. You are not being unsporting. And I hope that you do not think I am being unsporting in showing you what is a most effective imitation of a squid that is capable of being fished with a fly rod.

With the steady increase in the numbers of those who wish to tie their own flies, and the steady reduction in the availability of natural materials, there is bound to be an increase in the use of man-made materials in fly construction. In many of the more affluent countries in the world there are people who call themselves conservationists, and who are hell-bent on preventing you obtaining feathers and furs for fly-dressing. They have done it already with seal's fur. They have done it with many now-protected species of bird. The restrictions will multiply in future. But it will still be necessary for anglers to follow the rules, if there are rules, about what they may or may not tie onto the end of their leaders when they think they are fly fishing. Even if there are no rules, each of us must make up our own mind about what constitutes a lure that is acceptable to our own conscience. If in doubt, ask. Don't say I didn't warn you!

8. HOW SHOULD I FISH?

In this chapter I discuss some aspects of actual fishing. What you do at the waterside can make a vital difference. All the expertise at the fly-tying vice can be set at nought if you do not show your fly to the fish in a way that will entice a take.

Think of the average salmon angler – not the lucky person who lives a short distance from the waterside, who is retired, and who can drop the lawnmower and rush to the banks when he thinks the conditions are right! The average salmon angler plots and schemes, pores over his diary, and books a fishing trip months ahead. When he arrives at the waterside, the river can be a roaring flood, or so low that every pebble on the bottom is clearly visible. It is highly unlikely that he will arrive one day after a spate that has filled the river with taking fish. One year in ten, if he is fortunate, these God-given conditions will apply but normally his first glance at the river will fill him with despair. The ghillie will meet him with the words, 'It's a damned shame you weren't here last week' or, at the end of a week, will say, 'What a pity you cannot stay a few more days'!

Having flogged away for a ten-hour day, our holiday angler should consider what he has achieved. He may well, if it is a reasonable salmon river, at a reasonable time of the season, have shown his fly to a hundred salmon. On a famous river, in prime time, this figure could be multiplied several times. Why should an angler have a silly grin of satisfaction on his face if he has persuaded one salmon to take his fly? Or having fished hard for six days, and shown his fly to perhaps six hundred salmon in total, should he be pleased if he ends the week with one salmon? Yet this is exactly what the great majority of holiday salmon-anglers feel. One salmon per week is an average to which many anglers would aspire.

Occasionally, one has a red-letter day – a day when one has only to chuck any old fly into a pool and a salmon will grab it. Everyone up and down the river is catching fish that day. Yet they are the same anglers who had a blank the day before, and will have another blank the day after. Why? It can have nothing to do with skill. The same skill was used on both the red-letter day and on the blank day.

It cannot honestly be anything to do with the tackle – that was the same on both days. The fly or flies were the same too, so it cannot have anything to do with the angler. It all depends on the fish. What on earth can it be that causes lots of salmon to think one day that they do not feed in fresh water, and the next day to change their minds and have a go at anything that moves over their heads? Perhaps if we knew the true answer to this question we would stop salmon fishing, as it would become too predictable.

I remember, years ago, reading a book by the late Reg Rhygini called *Salmon Taking Times*. The book was a best-seller and is still in demand. I read it avidly from cover to cover, and failed to grasp the secret. I read it again, and again, and – apart from deducing that Reg had a theory that oxygen levels and light levels had something to do with it – I failed to be able to predict when a taking time would occur. Reg was a lovely man, looking at a Game Fair as if he had stepped out of a band-box, so impeccably turned out was he. He was a good casting instructor who took endless pains to get things right for his pupils, and a dedicated grayling angler. Yet I am assured that when he went salmon fishing, he fished from dawn to dusk just like the rest of us. Hedging his bets, he called it, and I am certain that he was right. However one may plot and scheme, take temperatures, look at the clouds, read the weather forecast, the only thing that makes a difference in today's state of the art is to get that fly in the water and keep it there, hour after hour.

By all means listen to the ghillie. He knows the river better than you know your own front garden. Not only does he know what the bottom looks like – all its nooks and crannies – he knows where the lies are. He knows where someone's fly was when a fish took it. If he has been on that beat for more than perhaps ten seasons, he will have seen hundreds of salmon caught, at all heights of the water. He will have formed a picture of where takes are most likely. Fish where the ghillie tells you to.

To start with – only to start with. After a few hours you will be ready to experiment. You will be able to try other places and the ghillie will not be offended by this. If you ignore his advice right from the beginning, he will walk away muttering to himself that he has another clever Dick here who doesn't need his help. If you form a thinking partnership with him, it will brighten his day and he will devote total attention and all his experience to helping you to catch a fish.

How often have you heard about the party of experienced anglers on a famous beat? Blank by the Wednesday, one of them asks the ghillie if he would be so kind as to try teaching his wife to fish. The woman is usually good-looking when this scenario is acted out! Off go the pair of them, ghillie carrying the rod, and lady beginner following. They disappear upstream into the trees, and return after an hour with a fish! The tackle was the same as was being used by the rest of the party. The fly came out of the ghillie's hat, where it had reposed untouched for the last three days. The fly just might have made a difference, but the essential difference was that the lady beginner did exactly as she was told – she didn't know any better. And they were probably fishing in a spot known to the ghillie as a reliable taking lie. Experience on the part of the ghillie put the beginner's fly in exactly the right spot, at the right depth, and at the right speed.

What was the right spot, depth, and speed? The same as had caught fish there before, and that man knew it. So listen to the ghillie. Regard him not as a servant who will put the tackle together for you at the beginning of the day, but as a partner: a partner who has more experience than you could possibly have. Day after day, year after year, he has to stand on the bank of perhaps a mile of river, watching people trying to catch fish without knowing where those fish are. He knows where they are. He knows where the fish are that are most likely to take a fly. And if you hand him the rod and suggest he has a go, it is remarkable how often he will tie into a fish while your jaw drops in astonishment.

This level of skill is made up of several factors: knowing exactly where the fish is lying, and at what depth; knowing just the speed of travel that has proved in the past to be attractive to fish lying there; and making the fly move in a way that has caught fish in the past. All these factors can be lumped together under one word – experience.

Imagine that you are standing beside the first pool of the day. Try turning to the ghillie and asking him to forget that you have fished here before. Ask him to give you a running commentary on what your fly should be doing and where. Have him stand close beside your left elbow if you are right-handed, and talk your fly through the pool. You may well be amazed at the way he will describe how your fly is moving too fast in that little eddy there, or drifting too slowly like a dead leaf here. Try suggesting another line mend to slow the fly down, or a gentle pull of line over the forefinger to speed the fly up, and see what he says. Follow his advice to the letter. Remember that, while you are on holiday, the ghillie is at work.

Circumstances can make work enjoyable, or it can be a drag. The difference in many cases is the level of challenge. If you become totally absorbed in a challenging aspect of work, the time flies by. To a ghillie, there can be a challenge, a mental drive, to get a salmon to take your fly. Or there can be days of utter boredom while some holiday anglers persist in doing their own thing, ignoring advice, creating the firm impression in the ghillie's mind that no fish will be caught. It is at this stage that one tends to swop stories, to talk about other things. This should be the warning bell that all is not well. If you are both, as a partnership, concentrating on trying to catch fish, there will not be any mental capacity left to remember jokes.

You might well start to talk to the fish. I know one ghillie who talks to the fish all the time the fly is doing what he wants it to do. 'C'mon, fishy, c'mon', is repeated over and over – an excellent sign that he is thinking fish, that his mind is fixed underwater, where that fly is flickering around in the currents in a tempting fashion. Which brings us to that fly underwater. How should it move?

If you believe the fishing books, or most of them, you will believe that a salmon fly should swim smoothly across the river, at a constant speed and depth, not too fast and not too slow. The bigger the fly, the faster should it move. The darker the fly, the nearer the surface should it be – and lots of other rules I have heard or read, none of which I regard as necessarily true.

What kind of fly have you tied on the end of your leader? If it is a tube fly or Waddington, do you think it represents a little fish? If so, do little fish swim smoothly at a constant speed for 18 m (20 yd) across a current that varies in speed from one side of the pool to the other? Of course they don't. Little fish usually swim in stops and starts unless they are part of a large shoal that has a herd instinct to be somewhere else. A little fish on its own must be terrified that it is going to be eaten at any moment. It sprints a metre or two, then pauses to look around, making sure that there isn't a pair of huge jaws poised near. Then it dashes again, then another pause, and so on. Surely, to simulate a little fish, therefore, one's fly should move in similar, short dashes, followed by a pause every now and again?

This can be achieved by pulling in line over the forefinger, then letting it pay out in the current, then pulling again. Not too fast nor too jerkily – remember the size of your fly: imagine it is in fact a little fish, and think of the speed attainable by a fish of that size in a current of that speed. Focus your brain on that fly. Keep thinking. Notice how the current speeds up as it comes around that rock? If the current is going faster, your fly should move over the ground more slowly, so that its swimming speed in the water remains exactly as you want it.

Can you hover the fly tantalisingly in front of the salmon's nose? By holding the rod out over the river, it is often possible for the fly to be made to hang motionless over the lie, flickering slightly from side to side in the whorls of the current. Salmon sometimes find this irresistible, particularly in the neck of a pool in the fast water. If there is a big rock at the head of the pool, it is sometimes feasible to sit comfortably, letting the fly skate on the surface of the fast water, back and forth across the current. Called dibbling, this technique seems to be most successful with a long fly, like a Collie Dog or Brook's Sunray fly. I have seen salmon come up through 1.8 m (6 ft) of fast water to take a dibbled fly – the rod was held by someone who could not cast, an absolute tyro.

Supposing you have a fly on the leader that, in your mind, is intended to look like a little prawn or shrimp. How do they move? Surely in a jerky progression, not in a long, smooth swim across and down. Have you thought that the river wet-fly trout-angler, gently flipping his rod-tip up and down as the fly swings round, is trying to impart exactly the sort of movement to his fly that your prawn should have? Then why has this form of twitching of the tip never caught on among salmon anglers? I wonder. Surely it is logical to assume that, if a little nymph swims this way, an enlarged version, in other words, a prawn or shrimp, will also swim that way? The difference of size between the nymph and the shrimp can be accounted for by the greater length of the salmon rod, and its consequent longer but slower flip of the rod tip. I commend to you that you give this some thought next time you are standing there watching your fly swim smoothly across a pool.

We can now consider the direction you cast. Most of the literature says that one should cast down and across, say at forty-five degrees to the flow of the current. Can you imagine a salmon lying there, seeing fly after fly travelling in exactly the same direction? I know that occasionally a salmon will have a mental breakdown and grab a fly, but if you are to *entice* a salmon to grab that fly, might it not pay you to do something different – like casting square across and letting the fly drag in short pulls across the current? Anything moving against the current *must* be alive. If it is alive it is probably edible: the food motive we talked about earlier.

In calm water it often pays to pull line in while the fly swims round. In other words, you are trying to convey the impression of positive movement by the fly – it looks as if it is actually going somewhere and, therefore, it must be alive. I have tried this in the past and found that sometimes a bow-wave appears behind the fly as a salmon follows it, perhaps 15 cm (6 in) behind. Slow down and the fish turns away immediately, losing interest. Speed the fly up, on the other hand, and you appeal to the predatory instinct of the salmon and it will grab that fly. There is also a possibility that a salmon that follows a fly like this is smelling it. We know they have an incredible sense of smell.

By speeding the fly up you allow aggression, or the urge to eat, to overcome the caution or curiosity that caused the salmon to follow the fly, smelling it. It is almost as if the thought process was 'I had better grab it before it gets away'. Fish that take the fly after following it are often well hooked, as they turn away against the pull of the line and hook themselves as they do so.

On hard-fished association waters it pays to remember that, if every angler takes the mandatory pace between casts, each salmon will see every fly three times, at least: once 1.8 m (6 ft) away, next cast 0.9 m (3 ft) away, next cast overhead. If ten anglers follow each other down a pool in an hour, every salmon has seen a total of thirty flies, at least. In clear water it might even be double that. If every angler is doing the same thing, is it any wonder that the fish get bored and go to sleep?

Might this be the reason for the infuriating success sometimes enjoyed by total beginners? They do not follow the rules because they do not know the rules – hence their flies do something different. The difference is enough to trigger a take by fish that have ignored everything else for hours or even days. It pays to try something different occasionally, but you will obtain more satisfaction if you think it out and have a reason for doing that something different. Then you can tell yourself that superior intellect put that salmon on the bank, and that luck had nothing to do with it!

We now come to the end of each cast. The fly has fished around in whatever manner you like, and the line is now pointing straight downstream from you. This is called 'on the dangle'. Many anglers miss the golden opportunity this position represents, and start the action of making the next cast. What about the fish lying down there, under the dangling fly? It merely sees the fly come around in the current, hang for a split second, then disappear off through the surface almost at the speed of sound.

If, on the other hand, you pull line in slowly over your forefinger for perhaps 1.8 m (2 yd), your fly will appear to swim straight upstream against the current for that distance. Therefore it must be alive. Therefore it must be edible. Very many salmon are caught by anglers who know how to pull the fly gently upstream from the dangle. One word of caution. If you pull like this when your fly is dangling below you, and you get a take, you will feel a sudden pull, or a dead weight. It might feel like a heavy jerk. *Do not strike.* Remember that the fish is likely to be facing directly towards you and a strike will whip the fly straight out of the salmon's mouth. You must let the fish turn away before lifting the rod and feeling for a hookhold. Better still is to dump the 1.8 m (2 yd) of line you have just pulled in and let the current drag this slack line below the fish, drawing the hook into the scissors as it does so. I must stress that to strike on the dangle is a recipe for disaster.

We now consider the predicament of the holiday angler, fishing a beat on which there is no ghillie. The hotel owner has told you where to park the car, or has given you a map showing the named pools, and told you to get on with it. Where do you start? Assume you approach the water and find a pool where there is a current coming in at the head of the pool, which flows against the opposite bank. On the opposite bank there is a steep cliff down into the water, with trees on top of it. Lower down the pool, the current smooths out, and there is an area of almost stationary water before the water again speeds up in a glide over the shallow sill into the rapids below – a typical salmon pool. The short answer, if you are a stranger, is to comb every centimetre of that pool, from the tumbling white water at the head, right over the sill into the rapids below. And if it is high summer and hot, it may well pay you to fish down the rapids too.

If you are lucky enough (or skilful enough!) to hook a salmon, remember where your fly was when it took – correct to one square centimetre. Then when you have calmed down after the battle, admired your fish, and laid it somewhere safe, get back to that same spot and try there again. You must realise that you have discovered a taking lie – a spot on the bottom of the river that is favoured by a salmon that may be in the mood to take a fly. You have just caught the previous occupant of that lie, and another fish may well move into the same place. A fish that has just moved is, for some reason, more likely to be a taker than is a fish that has been asleep for a week. Only when you are satisfied that you have combed the area of that lie without result should you move on in your covering of the pool. Then try that lie again in an hour.

I have found that, the longer the rapids between pools, the more likely am I to find a taking fish at the tail of the pool at the top of the rapids. It is as if the fish, swimming up the fast water, comes to a pool, eases itself over the sill, and stops for an immediate rest. If you are lucky, you present your fly to those fish before they go to sleep, and the very best place for this is right on the sill or lip of the pool. I have caught salmon right on the lip of a waterfall, where they almost had to risk being washed over as they rose to the fly. The fly, on one occasion I remember vividly, was skating on the surface at considerable speed before the last 0.9 m (3 ft) of leader disappeared over the

74

falls. Never neglect the lip of the pool, even if you can see every pebble on the bottom, and fish right out every last centimetre.

I have not so far mentioned depth. I am well aware that there is a rule that one uses a sinker below 7°C (45°F) water temperature, and a floater if the water is warmer. I do not think that the rule is as rigid as that. Certainly, salmon seem to be sluggish in very cold water: they will not run as far as they will in warmer water, and they are more reluctant to jump waterfalls if the water is cold. There is a very good reason for this. The temperature of the seas around the British coast does not vary very much. In the depths of winter the sea temperature is around 8°C (46°F). I am not talking about the occasional bitter spell that can freeze the sea near the beaches, but the average winter temperature of the bulk of the sea water around the northern half of the British Isles. At the end of a hot summer, it might just reach 15°C (59°F). In other words, a salmon entering one of Britain's rivers, say in February, will leave salt water at a temperature of 8°C (46°F) and enter fresh water that may be as cold as 2°C (35°F). No wonder it feels frigid and sluggish! I would feel the same.

Once the river water rises above 8°C (46°F), the salmon will feel warmer than it did at sea. Because it is a cold-blooded creature, its metabolism is dictated by its temperature, which in turn is dictated by its surroundings. So, up to a point, the warmer it is, the more active it is. That point is somewhere in the upper teens Centigrade (60s Fahrenheit) at which temperature the water begins to hold less free oxygen.

There is, therefore, a good, practical reason for salmon not to want to move far for a fly if they are very cold. In conditions like this, it does pay to get that fly deep, so that it wafts past the very noses of the fish. However, once the water temperature rises above the magical 7–8°C (mid-40s°F) it is surprising how far a salmon will travel on occasion to take a fly. I have seen salmon come vertically through 3.5 m (12 ft) of water to take my fly. Equally, on one day of baking hot weather and a water temperature in the upper teens Centigrade (mid-60s Fahrenheit), I caught fish on a fast sinking line that had refused all the normal 'greased-line' tactics.

On this day, on the Alness, I stood at the head of the pool and cast straight down the current, which flowed along under my bank. I let the line sink, then brought the fly straight upstream along the bottom in 15-cm (6-in) twitches. I had two fish in the hour or so I was trying this method. The fly was small, perhaps a 10, and bright orange with a gold body (see the shrimp pattern on p. 166). It was one of those lovely days when the countryside seemed to be asleep in the heat, and only trout and salmon parr were moving.

There are, therefore, no hard and fast rules about depth – at least none that hold good *all* the time, so again, experiment. If it feels warm, and the water feels warm, try first near the surface. If that doesn't work, change the line and try a slow-sinker or a sink-tip. If that doesn't work, put on a fast-sinker and get that fly down deep. It is easier to ring the changes on fly size first, of course, and that is as far as most people get. They feel they are too busy fishing to stop and re-thread the rod with a different line. Truth to tell, they are too busy fishing to think.

Now let us consider the leader to which the fly is tied. It does make a difference, as I found out to my cost last year. Consider two anglers, on a famous beat of a famous river, with lots of fish splashing about to keep interest at its peak. Both anglers are using 4.5-m (15-ft) carbon rods, and both are using the same colour of slow-sinking line. Both use similar flies. Both cast about the same distance from the boats. The boatmen, both highly experienced on the beat, swopped places each day so that each angler fished with a different companion on alternate days.

On the first day, I caught one salmon. My opposite number caught four. On the second day, I caught one coloured hen-fish that was returned. My opposite number caught five, all fresh fish like bars of silver. That is a total of nine fish for him and two for me – and I consider that a statistically significant difference. No fluke, no luck, no chance could cause a discrepancy of that amount.

Analysing the differences between us later, there was only one: I was using 10-kg (22-lb) nylon, which appeared to be quite clear in colour, but had a glittery surface. He was using 6.8-kg (15-lb) nylon, darker in colour than mine, and with less shine to the surface. I am quite convinced that this was the only difference and it must have caused the vast dissimilarity in our results. I vowed then that I would pay much more attention to my nylon. I would in future use nylon strong enough, of course, but not so strong that the salmon might be deterred from taking my fly. How strong does the nylon need to be?

Take a fairly typical 4.5-m (15-ft) carbon-fibre salmon fly-rod. Apply maximum strain in a heave. This maximum strain is applied with the rod held fairly low. If the butt is held upright, the rod groans and creaks alarmingly at a pull of 1.4 kg (3 lb). With the butt held low, perhaps thirty degrees above the horizontal, the maximum pull on the leader is about 2.3 kg (5 lb). You may well disbelieve these figures, but I can assure you that I have just tested them with a spring balance.

The amount of pressure I was applying to the rod handle, of course, was very much greater than these figures would suggest. My arms started to tremble with the effort when I was pulling with the butt low, but short of actually breaking the rod, I could apply no more.

What does this have to do with the strength of the leader? If it is impossible to apply more strain than a 2.3-kg (5-lb) pull on a leader, is there any justification, ever, for using nylon much stronger than this? Allowing for the reduction in strength caused by knots (and a badly-tied knot will reduce the strength of nylon by perhaps 50 per cent) and allowing for a jerk being applied when the fish shakes its head, it seems reasonable to assume that 4.5-kg (10-lb) breaking strain nylon will be perfectly strong enough for all normal salmon fishing. Then we have the person who likes to allow a safety margin in case the leader is rubbed against rocks while playing a fish. This person may well feel happier with 6.8-kg (15-lb) nylon. But the problem of jagged rocks applies to very few salmon rivers, most of which have rocks polished smooth by thousands of years of rushing water.

The size of the fly to be cast might also make a difference. A big brass tube fly is a pig to cast at any time. Tied to the end of fine nylon, a tube tends to misbehave in a terrifying manner, much like a brick tied to a piece of string. Equally, if a backcast is mis-timed, and the fly is still travelling backwards when the forward cast is begun, the fly applies a great strain to the leader. An 8-cm (3-in) brass tube fly weighs about 7 g (½ oz), and when it is flying through the air at a hundred miles an hour, and is suddenly reversed to a

77

hundred miles an hour in the opposite direction, the weight is multiplied many times, and nylon can part with a crack like a pistol shot if a cast is mis-timed. Even so, 6.8-kg (15-lb) nylon should be strong enough if care is taken with casting, however heavy the fly.

I have, therefore, made a vow to use finer nylon in future for my salmon fishing. Even if I want to lean back and *heave* when I am playing a fish, I know that it is physically impossible to apply more than a 2.3-kg (5-lb) pull. Having said that, there is one consequence of which I must be aware: nylon can weaken in use. I have also vowed to check my leader more often – always to put on a new leader each morning, and again at lunchtime. I know that if I neglect this precaution, I shall be broken by a fish sooner or later, and it will be entirely my own fault. And if I get a wind knot (caused by too much effort in casting, and not by the wind!) I shall stop immediately and replace the leader. It is a recipe for disaster to neglect this.

Nothing I have said about the strength of the leader, however, will make any difference if I have a foot on my flyline when a fish takes, or if the line is tangled around the reel handle! I tend to glance down and check everything after every cast, and by holding the line under the little finger of my upper hand I tend not to get tangles of line around the butt.

I come now to one last aspect of salmon fishing I want to discuss: wading. It seems that average anglers do not think they are fishing properly unless they are getting their wellies wet! Stillwater anglers suffer from this lemming-like instinct to wade. Salmon anglers seem to suffer from the same syndrome.

I have seen anglers approach a salmon pool, crunch along the shore in their heavy boots from one end to another, and then wade straight in at the head of the pool to knee depth, stop, and then – and only then – take the fly off the keeper ring and prepare to make the first cast. What happened to that old-fashioned word fieldcraft? What makes those anglers forget that a salmon is a wild creature, easily frightened? Why is it that they have to wade at all?

Give those same anglers a rifle and suggest that they might stalk a roe deer, and they will creep slowly and silently like a Red Indian. Put a salmon rod into their hands and they will slosh around in waders quite happily. And I would suggest that both wild creatures, the deer and the salmon, are very easily frightened. Frightened fish stop eating. Self-preservation is the strongest single instinct in all creatures. I fully realise that on the big four British salmon rivers it is frequently necessary to wade in order to cover the lies. I would humbly suggest, however, that on the great majority of salmon rivers in Britain, a reasonable caster can cover the width of the river without wading at all.

A few pages back I told the story of the wife being taken by the ghillie to catch a fish. I said then that the key to her success was that she did what she was told. Equally it might be true that she did not wade. Wearing either shoes or knee-high wellingtons, she may well have stood on the bank, and not frightened the fish before it saw her fly! Her husband, on the other hand, wearing the obligatory chest waders, might well have made every fish in the pool aware of his presence before he even unhooked the fly from its keeper ring!

I heard some little time ago of the man who was puzzled by the fact that every fish on his side of the river, for at least a couple of hundred metres downstream, stopped all activity as soon as he waded into the water. If you have ever sat in the sunshine and smelt the almost overpowering smell of rubber from a pair of waders, you might wonder if the fish might not also smell those waders as soon as they are put into the water it is breathing. We know that salmon have a highly-developed sense of smell, so why should the smell of rubber, or the smell of a human being, not reach them downstream of an angler wading? And most salmon fishing is done downstream from the angler.

So for several reasons it is a good idea not to wade. Wading frightens fish. The smell may well put them off. And there is a good prospect that an angler wading down a pool is wading over the lies of fish, frightening them sufficiently to make them dash off and convey their fear to other fish in the pool. Don't wade unless you really must, and then wade as if you are treading on eggs – gently.

I have just said that most salmon fishing is done downstream from the angler. I know a man, an excellent salmon fisher who, in low-water conditions, fishes a small fly upstream, just like an upstream nymph. He catches far more than his share of salmon – in fact, he catches salmon in conditions most people would regard as hopeless, and in hot, bright conditions his upstream nymph technique is looked on as a marvel by those who have seen him doing it. He wades, if he wades at all, as if he is gliding through the water at a centimetre a minute, and he wears felt-soled waders for silence on the stones of the bottom. He is good angler, a thinking angler, and an example to many of us.

In bright weather conditions, reconnaisance pay dividends. Find a high bank, and look from it into the river. Spot the fish lying in the pool, and register in your mind where they are. Fish your fly to the noses of those fish. Simple triangulation will help you to fix their positions – a straight line between a tuft of grass on this bank and a rock on the far bank, crossing another line between the light patch on the cliff over there and the depth gauge here, for example, will help you to pinpoint a fish. At least if you fish at a target fish you are not wasting time by fishing in empty water. In any salmon river there will be a lot of empty water.

At the end of this chapter, come back to the question, why should you be satisfied if you show your fly to one hundred salmon and only one of them takes it? Keep questioning every aspect of your fishing. If someone tells you something, inferring that it is a golden rule of fishing, ask them to prove it. If they cannot prove it to your satisfaction, try the theory out for yourself. If it works, all well and good. If it doesn't, tuck it away for another day – it might work in different conditions. Do not believe everything you read in books and magazine articles – salmon do not read them. Unless you hurl it into a river in disgust, the salmon will not read this book either!

9. SOME HINTS ON FLY-TYING

I should stress at the very beginning of this chapter that it is not aimed at the reader who has never tied flies before. For the necessary knowledge to enable you to start fly-dressing, or fly-tying, you should learn from a friend, from evening classes, or from books and magazine articles combined with struggling on your own. It is best to learn from a skilled practitioner as you will then pick up many short-cuts. If you are determined to start out on your own, be reassured that tying your own salmon flies is very easy.

Everything is on a larger scale than on trout flies, with nice, big hooks to lash materials onto. The materials themselves are much less fragile. And, if we do not know why a salmon takes a fly, how do we know what a good salmon fly looks like? It is all very well for the purists to stress that the tail and topping of a well-tied fly should meet in a point; that the hackle should reach only to the point of the hook; that ribbing should be evenly wound, with equal gaps between turns; and that heads should be small, and varnished with three coats of varnish to give a nice, glossy effect – all from the human standpoint. No one has asked a salmon what it thinks of such works of art.

From a human point of view, a fly should be durable. Materials should be well tied onto the hook or tube, so that the fly does not fall apart under the stresses of a hard day's fishing. The appearance should please the man behind the rod, or he will not fish as diligently, or with as much concentration and effort, as he should. Apart from those two basic attributes, the fly can be of any shape, size, or colour that pleases you – or your ghillie!

It does help if you have some basic idea in mind when you sit down at the vice. You must have a plan before you make the basic choice – hook or tube? Single, double, or treble? And what size? Once you have made that basic decision, it is only a matter of creating the shape and colour you have in mind. And, having said

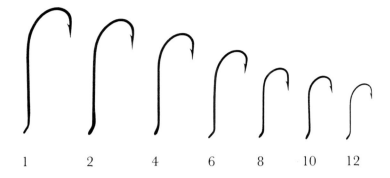

1   2   4   6   8   10   12

Salmon singles.

that, if you are one of those pernickety souls who count the hairs in the wing of a Hairy Mary before you buy it, this chapter is not for you!

There are those who get pleasure from every moment spent at the fly-tying vice. I am not one of them. I get pleasure from looking at the fly I have just created, but between dreaming it up and looking at the final article, there is the chore of tying it. Being basically lazy, I take every short-cut I can think of – not, I would hasten to add, at the expense of durability, as that must be paramount. But there are lots of little dodges that speed up the fly-tying process and enable me to produce ten flies an hour when my friends will produce only six flies in the same time. I reckon that this time-saving allows me either to ponder more about the design before I start, or to fill my flybox with more flies in the time available. And there never seems quite enough time to do everything I want to pack into a day anyway. I fancy that what I am really saying is that I do not get a thrill out of laying nice, even turns of silk along a hook. I get a thrill out of seeing the finished fly, and an even bigger thrill out of catching a fish on it. But the mechanics do not rank higher than perhaps tenth in my order of pleasures.

For this reason, I have work-studied the process of tying a salmon fly. I have watched perhaps the finest fly-dresser in this country, John Harris, drop a hair-winged salmon fly out of his vice every three or four minutes with a feeling akin to awe, and learned some of his short-cuts. I have spent many hours with him, talking about ways of doing things that might speed up the production of nice flies, and some of the ideas in this chapter are his.

Let us start with a discussion of the workplace itself. If you are very lucky, you will have a room set aside as a study, fly-tying room, fishing-book library, rod room, or whatever. If you are so lucky, I urge you to ban entry to the children unless accompanied by you, and to offer to do all the housework in there for yourself. There is nothing worse than a keen housewife, let loose in your room, who decides to 'tidy the mess up' for you. You will spend months looking for things! Better to have a pact. Volunteer to keep the place in a reasonably clean and tidy state, in return for her never going in there with a vacuum cleaner without your prior approval!

Organise your room so that you can leave a vice set up permanently on a bench. Then when you have an idea you can sit down straightaway and work on it. If you have to start by getting all the kit out, you will be inclined to defer the project until some other more suitable time, and you will forget that brilliant idea. Store all your materials in a logical order, well protected against moth or mite. It helps to be able to lay your hands on something without hunting around in drawer after drawer. Store your hooks in a logical order. Do not dump all your salmon singles into one box and comb

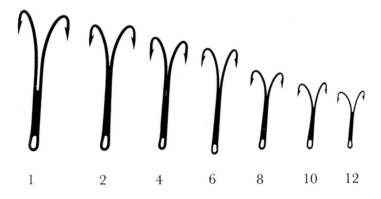

Salmon doubles.

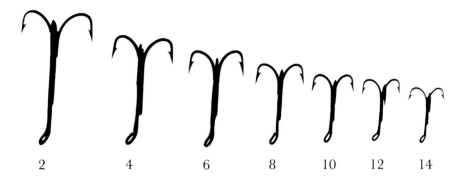

Esmond Drury trebles.

through each time you want a size 4 – all you will find is that you just ran out of 4s, and it is maddening.

If the vice is permanently set up there should be, lying beside it, your scissors, dubbing needle, hackle pliers, and varnish bottle. Items used on almost every fly, like silver and gold tinsel and black floss, should be in easy reach. The rest of the materials can be stored in drawers or boxes. An old writing-desk, full of cubbyholes, can be picked up quite cheaply at a local furniture auction, and makes a wonderful fly-tying desk and storage unit. Tidiness and organisation is all-important.

If you are one of the many unlucky souls living in a house full of people, without a spare room, you have to be even more tidy and organised. You may well have to tie flies on the kitchen table after the kids have been cajoled to bed. In this case, you will bless the day you made yourself a box to store everything in. Not just a box, but a box full of divisions and compartments, with a proper hinged lid and secure catches. This box can be put in the middle of the table, opened out, and there before you is an array of materials, stored in plastic bags, in logical order: all the tools in one compartment; all the tinsels in another; threads in another; hair in another; feathers for wings in another; feathers for hackles in yet another; and boxes of hooks in yet another. Got an idea of the number of compartments your box should have? Almost limitless. And by the time you have planned it properly, the box has grown to the size of a large suit-case!

Before you start tying flies on the kitchen table, find a cardboard box – a large one, like that whopper in which you carried the groceries out of the supermarket. Cut it all round to make a tray perhaps 20 cm (8 in) deep. Put it on the floor between your feet, and start tying flies. All the scrap you drop will fall into the tray, which can be searched for valuable hooks before tipping the scrap into the fire or dustbin at the end of the session. This is one way of avoiding vet's bills for the surgical operation of removing a treble hook from the dog's paw, or the wrath at a hook found jammed in the Hoover.

You are now ready to start. 'Take a length of thread,' the books say. I don't. I suggest you obtain a bobbin-holder with flared nozzle, and put the reel of thread into it. It is a great time-saver to buy at least six bobbin-holders, and put into them all the commonest col-ours of thread you use – floss too, and tinsel. We shall see why in a moment. (If you want to save money, do not buy a whip-finish tool – learn to do this knot by hand, it's quicker.)

Let us assume that you are going to tie a single-hooked or double-hooked Silver Blue, sometimes called a Teal, Blue and Silver. It's a nice simple fly, popular for salmon and sea-trout everywhere. Here, the books suggest that you start by running the thread along the shank in neat, touching turns until you reach the point where the tail and flat tinsel is going to be tied in. Don't bother – this is one tradition that is a waste of time.

Start with a bobbin-holder of flat silver tinsel. The kind I use is

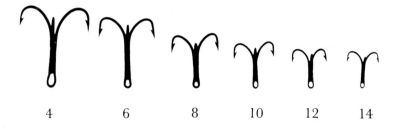

| 4 | 6 | 8 | 10 | 12 | 14 |

Tube-fly trebles.

double-sided – silver one side and gold the other – and, yes, it is in a flared bobbin-holder. Hold the waste end in your left hand and the bobbin-holder in your right (if you are right-handed), and start winding at a point where the wing roots are going to be, working back towards the tail. Do not worry if you leave gaps here and there. When you have wound perhaps ten or twelve turns, let the bobbin-holder hang, and the twists will unwind themselves while you reach for the scissors and clip away any waste end. The bobbin-holder will actually over-wind itself, and start spinning backwards again. Grab it when it has stopped turning, before it reverses the way it was untwisting, and you will have accumulated some twists in the tinsel so that you can wind next time perhaps fifteen times before having to let go again. You have a small credit balance of twists, so to speak. When you reach the tail-end of the body, take the golden pheasant topping-feather you laid on the bench beforehand, and tie it on top of the body with the tinsel. You will notice that I said nothing about stripping the feather to remove the fluff – I do not do this, but tie in the whole feather just as it was plucked from the head of the bird. If the feather is large enough to protrude the correct amount to form the tail, and have the waste end long enough to lie along the whole of the body, then great, I shall not get a bump in the tinsel body.

Having tied the tail in, I can also tie in a length of silver oval or wire if I want an over-ribbing. Make sure the waste end is long enough to reach the wing roots, then again, no bump under the tinsel body. Carry on winding the flat tinsel back along the body until the starting point is reached, and let the bobbin-holder hang. Only now do I reach for my thread in its own bobbin-holder, wind a few turns to start it, winding over itself at a point just ahead of the end of the tinsel, and break the waste end away by jerking it forward over the eye of the hook. Reaching for scissors is a waste of time – break it off.

Then the thread is wound behind the hanging tinsel two or three turns and, resting the thread bobbin-holder on the back of my left hand while the fingers of my left hand are holding the tinsel bobbin, I reach for my scissors and cut the tinsel. This avoids the scissors cutting both tinsel and thread, immediately after which I will swear in disbelief while the whole fly leaps undone.

If I have tied in a ribbing material, I will now leave the thread hanging, and wind the ribbing up the body. There are two schools of thought here – one says to wind in the opposite direction to the tinsel, so that the two materials cross over each other. In my opinion this tends to loosen the turns of flat tinsel, so I always wind in the same direction. If I am greatly bothered about sheer durability, I would put a lick of varnish over the tinsel body at this stage, and let it dry while I prepare the hackle and wings. This is one of those silly things people argue about – you are not necessarily wrong, just different from the other person, and you are both entitled to your opinions. As long as you have a logical reason for doing it your way, you ain't wrong!

Hackle next. Some people believe that a hackle should be wound, then drawn down and held rearwards by more turns of thread. What do I do? I reach for a bleached and dyed squirrel-tail in a nice, rich-blue colour, cut a bunch of hair, hold it by the tips and stroke out the fluff and short hairs, offer it to the hook in my right hand to judge the length, reach over with my left hand to hold it, take the bobbin-holder in my right hand, and take a couple of loose turns of thread around both shank and hair. Take my left hand away and tighten the thread. If it doesn't look right, shove it around a bit until it is, then take another few turns to secure it. It takes less time to do than it took you to read this, I can assure you.

What do I gain by using hair instead of feather for a hackle? Apart from time, I also save money. If I have a bleached and dyed squirrel-tail, I can use it for the hair on tubes, for wings on hooks, and for hackles on hooks. I cannot remember the last time I used that nice, dyed cock-cape in a teal-blue colour that cost me several pounds. Squirrel tails are actually cheaper than cock capes, and I defy anybody to tell that my hackles are not made of feathers.

Take the prepared teal slips – whether you double them, or use four separate slips, or just two, is up to you – and tie them on top of the hook shank with a pinch-and-loop. Do several pinch-and-loops. Then take your left fingers away while saying a little prayer, and if you have been good, your wings will look like the illustration of the Silver Blue later in the book. If you haven't been good enough for the gods to smile on you, you will see a horrible mess where the wings should be. Best to chuck them away and start again. When you are happy with the wings, reach for your scissors and trim off all the waste ends of hackle and wings. Do this at the same time, do not reach for the scissors, trim hackles, put the scissors down and start on the wings, and then go through it all again after the wings. Do it once, and clean up everything before you wind the head.

Having wound the head to the fatness you like (or slimness you read about!), reach for your half-hitch tool. This is an old Biro pen with the guts removed. Take one turn of thread around the point of this, offer it over the eye, and slip the knot off onto the head. Now do three more of these lightning knots. Take the scissors, form a long, thin V with the blades, and push the V onto the thread while holding it tight. The blades will cut the thread, but will brush aside all other materials that are not under tension. Now take the varnish bottle, with its brush in the lid, and put a good blob of varnish all round the head. Not quite so much as will run into the eye of the hook, but a good, sloshing helping. Take the fly out of the vice and stick the hook into a small piece of foam on the edge of your fly-tying bench, so that the shank is lying horizontal. If the eye points down, the varnish will run into the eye – if it is horizontal, the varnish will accumulate on the underside of the head.

If you believe those who say that a fly is not properly tied without a whip finish, by all means tie one before cutting the thread, but in all the years I have been fishing with my own flies, I have never had a single fly come apart because my three or four half-hitches and a good blob of varnish have failed. Hackles may have come unwound when flies have been belted on stones in the backcast, tinsel may have been cut by the teeth of a kelt, but never has the head come undone.

I think I ought to say here that, when I am running a fly-tying class, I show my pupils how to do a whip finish by hand, but then I also show them my quick way, and future decisions are up to them. It is not a question of 'do what I say, not what I do'. I explain the merits of both methods as far as I am aware, and then let them make up their own minds.

I have standardised on clear fly-head varnish. I no longer use black, as it is only too easy to dab some of this onto light-coloured hackle or wings, and the result is a mess. If I want a black head, and tradition says I should on nearly every fly, I put clear varnish onto black thread and the head looks black – and no risk of a shaky hand making a muck of things. If I want a red head, I use red thread with clear varnish on top, or even an overlay of fluorescent red floss on the head before the clear varnish.

When I start a new bottle of varnish, I leave the lid off for twelve hours, allowing some of the solvents to evaporate off. This thickens the varnish to the point where it will not drip off the brush onto my trousers with the ease with which new, runny varnish does. Once the varnish achieves the necessary viscosity, however, I make sure that I put the lid on after every single time I use it. Then if the bottle is knocked over on the worktop, I have time to grab it before all the varnish runs out and, equally, it never becomes too thick to use before the bottle is exhausted. There is a happy medium for this thickness, and the average fly-dresser usually achieves it by accident when the bottle is about half-empty. The worst thing you can do is to leave the top off for the whole of each fly-dressing session – you will throw away more varnish than you will use because it has gone solid in the jar.

If I may come back to the tinsel: I now never use flat, metal tinsels. I know that they are stronger than the modern, plastic tinsels, and are cut by the teeth of fish to a much lesser degree, but they are pigs to work with, making it much more difficult to achieve a neat body, and they tarnish with age. Modern, plastic films with a vacuum film of glitter applied to their surfaces are faster to work with, and are durable enough for me, particularly if they are reinforced by a ribbing of wire or oval tinsel. As I said earlier, I have now standardised on Mylar two-tone flat tinsel, sold by Tom Saville, in a size he calls no. 12. It is 1.3 mm ($\frac{1}{20}$ in) wide, and goes through a flared bobbin-holder like a dream. This material has saved me hours and hours over the years.

We come now to the tying of tube flies. Many people make heavy weather of this simple task, usually because they read, and believe as gospel, everything said about this simple piece of handicraft. I should first like to discuss safety. Tying a tube fly is perhaps the most perilous job undertaken by the average fly-dresser. Every time my fly-tying classes start on tube flies, I have cause to shout and swear at the risks run by the unthinking.

Tube flies have to be held in something, and the usual drill is to find a needle of the correct size to jam inside the tube. The needle is then fixed in the jaws of the vice by its eye, and the tube slid onto the needle until it jams. I have seen people drop the tube just as they were about to slide it onto the needle, bend down to pick it up and, as they straighten up, miss the point of that needle with an eyeball by fractions of a centimetre. I shudder every time I see it and, in order to drive the safety lesson home, I bawl and shout at them. It is the only time I ever do this in a fly-tying class, but I cannot stop myself. The thought of somebody losing the sight of an eye in one of my classes is something I dare not contemplate.

There is a safe way. The needle should be fed into the tube in the fingers until the tube jams. Then the needle and tube together are offered to the jaws of the vice, and the jaws clamped over the eye of the needle. The tube can be tightened slightly with a twist, and is then held securely for the fly-dressing operation. When the fly is finished, the tube is slackened from the needle with a twist, then needle and tube together are removed from the vice jaws and separated in the fingers. Whatever you do, *never leave a needle sticking out of the vice jaws*. At the worst you will blind yourself. At best you will skewer yourself in the forearm as you reach across the bench for something.

Even with a normal hook in the jaws, if you drop something, put the left hand over the vice jaws and hook, bend down, picking up the item with the right hand, then after you have straightened up, remove the left hand from the vice. It is difficult to stab yourself in the eye with something you are gripping with the left hand.

However, having stressed the safety aspect, let us now consider the tying of a tube fly. Imagine that it is a Willie Gunn, a fly with a black floss body ribbed with flat or oval gold tinsel, and a wing of hair – a blend of three colours. Choose the length of tube you want, put it onto its needle or special holder, and put the needle or holder in the jaws of the vice so that the tube sits horizontally. Pick up your bobbin-holder loaded with black floss and, starting around the wing-root position, take the floss around the shank of the tube, winding back over the standing (or waste) end. Hold this waste end up at an angle, and every turn of floss will run downhill and end up as a touching turn with its predecessor. After half-a-dozen turns have locked the floss, you have a choice. You can reach for the scissors and cut off the waste end, or you can keep on winding until the waste end disappears under the turns along the body. For this to work, the waste end should have started short enough to be shorter than the length of the body in the first place. This also saves considerably on floss, as there is effectively almost no waste.

Consider the person who habitually cuts away a 10-cm (4-in) waste end of floss. He or she will use a total of 40 cm (16 in) of floss per tube fly, whereas I should use only 30 cm (12 in) for the same fly. From an 18-m (20-yd) spool of floss, they will tie forty-five flies and I will tie sixty. I feel that there is a real financial saving to be made here. Waste ends cost money, so leave the waste end as short as possible, and bury the end under the turns as you progress in a fast spiral towards the tail of the tube.

Arriving at the tail-end of the tube, let the bobbin-holder hang, and reach for the tinsel. This is also on a bobbin-holder, and the tinsel is tied in so that the waste end lies along the tube to the wing-root starting-point. This avoids a bump somewhere along the body where the tinsel ends, and I accept that I am using perhaps 2 cm (1 in) more tinsel than I need to! Take a few turns of floss to lock the tinsel in, and then allow the tinsel bobbin to hang, or drape it over the rear of the vice jaws out of the way, and continue winding the floss, slightly more carefully this time, back towards the front of the tube, covering any gaps in the first layer.

Reaching the starting-point, allow the floss bobbin to hang, and take up the tinsel bobbin. Wind the ribbing up the body in the spacing you fancy, and when you reach the wing-root starting-point, let this bobbin hang beside the other. It is at this stage that you pick up your thread bobbin for the first time. Start the thread immediately in front of the hanging ends of floss and tinsel, and when it is secure, break the waste end away with a smart flick of the left wrist forward over the front of the tube. Take the bobbin around underneath both floss and tinsel a couple of times, locking them onto the tube. Reach for the scissors, and holding the thread bobbin out of the way with the back of the left hand, hold the floss and tinsel bobbins by their nozzles with the fingers of that same hand. With the right hand holding the scissors, cut through the floss and tinsel, and lay the bobbins down, making sure that the cut ends do not migrate back into the spigots. You have a fiddly re-threading job to do if you neglect this precaution.

Take a few more turns of thread round the tube to secure any minor taggy ends of floss or tinsel, and to prepare a bed for the hair wing. If this bed is not the same diameter as the body floss, the hair will flare out too much, and the fly will not appear as sleek as you want it to.

Now pick up a bucktail or bleached and dyed squirrel-tail. You will need three of these for a Willie Gunn – one black, one yellow, and one orange. Cut a small pinch of hair from each, holding the bunch by its tips and then stroking out the fluff and short hairs. As each colour is prepared, lay it down so that the roots of the bunch protrude 13 mm (½ in) over the edge of the table. Lay the next bunch on top, and then the third. Pick them all up together, making sure the tips are level, and roll the whole bunch around between finger and thumb a few times. It will be found that the colours blend together, and you will now have a bunch of hairs nicely mixed, without clumps of any one colour predominating, and the tips will still be level. Lay the bunch down again, and with a dubbing needle or the points of your scissors, divide the bunch into two, nearly equal, parts. Pick up one of the parts, and offer it for length to the tube with the right hand. Once it is in the correct position, change the grip on the hair to that of the left hand, and take two loose turns of thread around the hair and tube together. Shove it around a bit until it seems to occupy about half of the circumference of the tube. Now pick up the other half of the hair and repeat the performance on the far side of the tube. Shove around a bit more until the hair seems evenly distributed round the tube, and then tighten up on the thread and take a few more turns for safety's sake.

Pick up the scissors and cut off the waste ends of the hair, but not too close – leave almost 6 mm (¼ in) of waste sticking out. Now stroke these short waste ends backwards with the fingers of the left hand, and take more turns of thread to hold them down. By the time you have kept on stroking waste ends back, and wound threads over them, you will have finished the head of the fly, all the waste ends are buried, and because the root of each hair is doubled back upon itself under the head, it will never pull out. You will have tied a really durable fly that will never moult its wing.

All that remains is to tie a few half-hitches, or a whip finish if you are finicky, and slosh the varnish on. If you used black thread and clear varnish, you will have a nice, shiny, black head. Now remember to take tube and needle out of the vice together!

A couple of points about hair that will make your fly-tying easier. It is most essential that you take the trouble to remove all the fluff and short hairs from a bunch before tying it onto a fly. This applies to all forms of attached hair, be they hair wings on a single or double, hackles on singles or doubles, or wings on a tube or Waddington. If all the hairs are not long, the wing will appear thicker than it should at the roots. The wing will not be as secure as it should be. And because the roots are bulkier, the hair will flare outwards and not lie sleekly along the body.

With bucktail, there is a slightly different problem. Bucktail as sold for fly-tying comes from a deer, and most of the hairs on a deer are hollow. This is a benefit if you are trying to spin deer hair as, when the thread crushes the hollow hair, it bends violently outwards at that point. Rather like a thin, metal tube, if it is creased across it will collapse. If used for a wing on a tube fly, this flaring is the last thing you want to happen, so most bucktail is unsuitable for use as a hair wing or hair hackle. The answer is to choose hairs from a bucktail that are much longer than you need, as much as twice as long. By tying the hair in half-way along its length, it will be found that the hair is not so hollow as it is at the roots, and it will tie in to lie sleekly. This does, of course, reduce the proportion of hair on a bucktail that you can use for hair wings to less than half, as the remainder of the hair will be too short and will be too hollowly constructed.

You can avoid this problem of flaring to a certain extent by taking the turns of thread very loosely around the base of the wing, and only tighten up on the thread after a few winds, and after leaving the flare point and working forwards. Flies tied with this dodge tend to fall apart very readily, however, as hollow hair is also brittle, and even if the hair does not pull out it will break off during the act of casting. The only safe way to tie durable hair wings with bucktail is to be ruthless and use only the tips of very long hair, discarding the butts into the box between your feet.

If you also tie trout flies, the hollow, shorter hairs make marvellous coloured Muddler heads, so there is no need to throw away a bucktail when you have used up all the very long hairs on your salmon tubes. Because the bucktail started white underneath you will have strong-dyed colours without the usual problems associated with ordinary-dyed deer hair, which has had all the substance taken out of it in the bleaching process and, as a result, never spins well.

I said at the beginning of this chapter that tying salmon flies is very easy. It is, but I have seen dedicated fly-dressers take half an hour to tie one fly – not a beauty with traditional married wings, butts, toppings, jungle-cock eyes, and so on, but a simple fly like a Hairy Mary. I reckon to dress a simple hair-wing fly in less than five minutes, and it will be indistinguishable in the box and while fishing from the one over which such care was taken. I urge you to forget all about touching turns of silk, wound-and-drawn-down hackles, and flies that are perfect in every minute detail, unless you really enjoy producing a work of art every time. I believe that I am tying flies to fish with, and nobody has ever asked a salmon to take part in the judging of a fly-dressing competition! I have, on the other hand, looked into someone's flybox and thought that the rows of feather jewellery displayed were too beautiful to fish with! Somewhere there must be a happy medium, and having given you some time-saving dodges, the decision about your future attitude to lashing bits of fur and feather onto a hook to deceive some stupid fish must be yours alone!

10. INTRODUCTION TO COLOUR SECTION

This section is not intended to be a 'me too' list of flies, nor is it intended to be a comprehensive list of classic salmon flies. It is intended to give the reader some food for thought – to encourage the fly-dresser to think about a fly before it is dressed in the same way it has always been dressed; to think what a pattern is supposed to represent; to think what a pattern will look like underwater; and to try new ways of doing things with hooks and fly-dressing materials.

On each page are shown several ways of looking at a pattern, or some similar patterns. A recipe for a fly can be read by six fly-dressers, and every one will produce a different effect, depending upon the working style, the proportions of material used, and the shape of the finished fly. And all will give a different impression underwater. Put some materials on a single hook, a double hook, a treble hook, or a tube or Waddington, and the end result will appear totally different.

If we *really knew* why a salmon takes a fly, the task of producing fish-catching flies would be made very much easier. But do we honestly want to remove the magic of uncertainty from salmon fishing? A study of the following pages, it is hoped, will encourage more experimentation among those who tie salmon flies for their own use.

It must be stressed that, where a pattern is shown dressed by the author on a single hook, this has been done because the resultant fly lies flat and, when photographed, the dressing is all in focus and shows up more clearly. The flies on single hooks that have been provided by other anglers and fly-dressers are those with which they are happy to fish. One person's meat . . . and I would not dream of saying they are wrong in using single hooks.

I shall be well pleased if, after reading this book, you go to your fly-tying vice and sit there for a moment with half-closed eyes, transporting your thoughts to a spot in the ocean fifty miles south of

Iceland where, 3.7 m (12 ft) below the surface in clear, green water, there swims a shoal of salmon, feeding on a cloud of krill. How can you dress a fly that, when moved properly, will trigger that feeding memory in the mind of the next salmon you cover with a fly? Think of the satisfaction you will feel if it takes your fly. You will feel that you earned that fish. There will be less 'chuck-and-chance-it' in your fishing.

Read through this colour section and then take yourself off to your fly-tying vice and have some fun experimenting. You fish for fun, don't you? You damn well shouldn't – you should fish to catch fish, and that happens to be fun!

COLOUR
REFERENCE
SECTION

SQUID

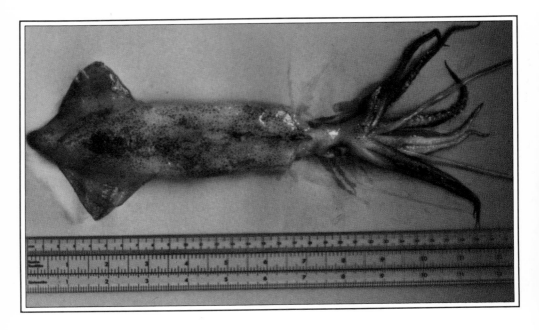

Fig. 1

Squid (Todarodes), *viewed from above.*
Notice that this specimen is 30 cm (1 ft) long, and the samples found in the stomachs were very much smaller.

SQUID

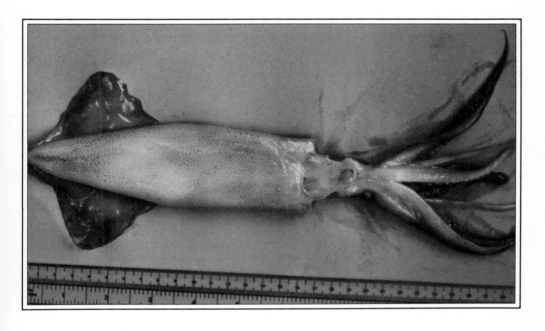

Fig. 2

*View showing the colour
from underneath. Squid can change colour very rapidly.
(Both photographs by courtesy of G. Howard.)*

SQUID

Squid (*Todarodes*). Many species change colour in less than a second. Normally a pale brown on top and cream coloured underneath, squid can change from white through yellow to orange, red and purple, almost to black.

The normal swimming speed for squid is slow but they can, when necessary, move very swiftly backwards by using water propulsion. They are the favourite food of many fish, from tunny to mackerel and whales.

The squid shown are over 30 cm (1 ft) in length, but those eaten by salmon average about 14 g (0.5 oz) in weight.

FISH

Sprat (*Sprattus sprattus*). The sprat shoals in summer at a depth of 10–50 m (10–55 yd) and in winter down to depths of 150 m (165 yd). The 'Golden Sprat' used for bait fishing for salmon is dyed, and does not occur in nature.

Sand-eel (*Ammodytes tobianus*) Shoals around the British Isles and in a band from Orkney to Iceland. Seldom found at depths greater than 30 m (33 yd), sand-eel are a favourite food of salmon.

Herring (*Clupea harengus*). Another favourite food for salmon. The main species spawns along the coast of Norway. The herring feed by sight, and thus mainly by day near the surface.

Pearlside (*Maurolicus muelleri*). Has light organs on underside. Found down to 150 m (165 yd) during the day, it comes to the surface at night.

Lantern fish (*Myctophidae*). Has light organs along the sides. Found deep during the day and at the surface at night. In a sample, 40 out of 48 salmon had eaten lantern fish.

Capelin (*Mallotus villosus*). Found mainly north of the Arctic Circle. By day they shoal at depths of about 150 m (165 yd), coming to the surface by night.

FISH

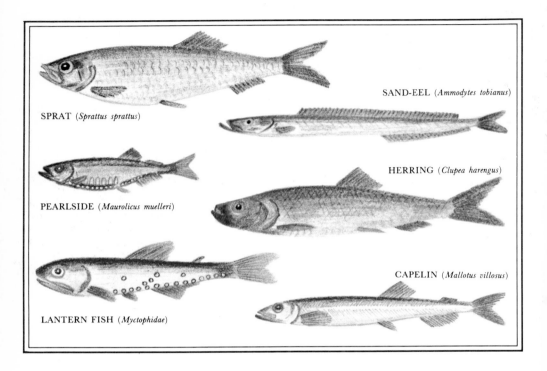

SPRAT (*Sprattus sprattus*)

SAND-EEL (*Ammodytes tobianus*)

PEARLSIDE (*Maurolicus muelleri*)

HERRING (*Clupea harengus*)

LANTERN FISH (*Myctophidae*)

CAPELIN (*Mallotus villosus*)

Fig. 3

These drawings are not to scale,
and are intended as a rough guide for the fly-dresser. Any of the fish pictured
here can be from 5 cm (2 in) long upwards.

SHRIMP, PRAWN AND COPEPOD

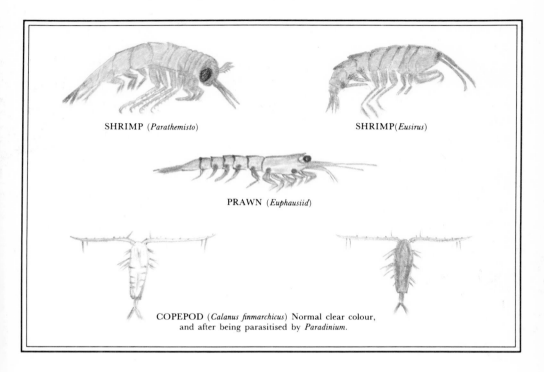

SHRIMP (*Parathemisto*)

SHRIMP(*Eusirus*)

PRAWN (*Euphausiid*)

COPEPOD (*Calanus finmarchicus*) Normal clear colour, and after being parasitised by *Paradinium*.

Fig. 4

Note*: these drawings should be
regarded as sketches for the fly-dresser, not as accurate drawings
for the student of marine biology!*

SHRIMP, PRAWN AND COPEPOD

Shrimp (*Parathemisto*) One salmon in a sample had over 1,700 para-themisto in its stomach, the total weight of which was just over 28 g (1 oz). Another seven salmon in the sample had over 1,000 in the stomach. A size-10 standard wet-fly hook would be the right size for dressing.

Shrimp (*Eusirus*) Similar to *Parathemisto* but larger – 25 mm (1 in). They would be correctly imitated on a single size-4 salmon hook. Not nearly as numerous as *Parathemisto* – the maximum found in a salmon stomach during a sample was five.

Prawn (*Euphausiid*) The *Euphausiid* found in the stomach of salmon are small, 0.14 g on average (or almost 200 to an ounce). In a sample almonst half the salmon tested had eaten *Euphausiid*, although the maximum number was six.

Copepod (*Calanus finmarchicus*). About the size of a grain of rice. Normally almost transparent, they turn bright red when invaded by the parasite *Paradinium*. Can be dressed on a size-14 hook.

SALMON FOOD

This is a photograph of food taken from the stomach of a salmon. The salmon was caught on a baited longline, north of the Faeroes, in March 1983, and the sample was kindly sent to me by John Hislop. The photograph is enlarged.

The top-left creature, a shrimp-like thing called an amphipod of the genus *Parathemisto*, is actually about 25 mm (1 in) long, and would correctly be imitated on a single salmon-hook size 4. As can be seen, the top-right shrimp is a bit smaller.

The bottom row is a tiny, prawn-like animal called a euphausiid, of the genus *Meganyctiphanes*. When laid out straight it is perhaps 19 mm (¾ in) long, and could be dressed to occupy the whole of the shank of a size-6 hook, or a size-8 longshank.

I am assured that the colour has not changed much from that of the creatures when they were alive. The formalin, and the digestive juices of the salmon, have resulted in a slight increase in opacity – the creatures looked more transparent when they were alive.

Have you ever seen a salmon fly that looked at all like these creatures? Why not?

SALMON FOOD

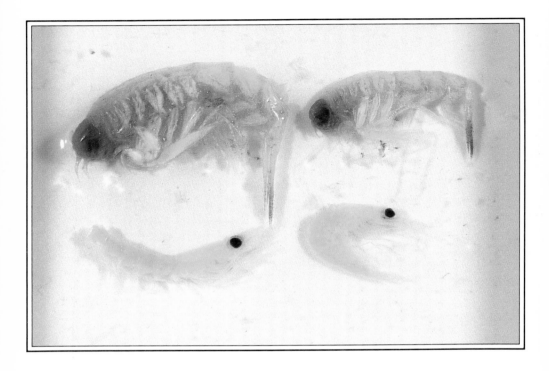

Fig. 5

Samples from the stomach of a
salmon shown magnified three times.
Shrimps (Parathemisto) – top
Prawns (Euphausiids) – bottom

Fig. 6

Waddington (top):
Single hook version (bottom left):
Drury treble (bottom right)

AKROYD

The Akroyd is a fly pattern well over a hundred years old. Apparently invented by Charles Akroyd of Brora, it was soon modified to have Dee-style strip wings dressed low over the body. There is now considerable confusion over the correct dressing, as various sources suggest, for the rear half of the body – yellow seal's fur, yellow floss, orange mohair, and, most recently, fluorescent orange floss. The wings have been variously suggested as cinnamon turkey, white turkey, or white hair!

The Waddington (top) is an original by Alexander Martin of Glasgow, where wool appears to have been used on both halves of the body. The wing is black heron, and the hackle is guineafowl. The yellow, palmered body hackle has faded a little over the years.

In my single-hook version (bottom left), I have used the tip of a scarlet cock's hackle instead of the Indian crow in the tail, and the wing should lie lower in true Dee style – if it did, it would hide the body, so I have cocked it up a little. The jungle-cock eye points downwards as suggested by Crosfield, and I have used a teal throat as also suggested by him. On the Drury treble (bottom right) I have used black bucktail and omitted the throat, to show how this old pattern can still be attractive despite simplification.

ARNDILLY FANCY

This is not one of the famous old patterns, but its cheerful attractiveness appeals to me and to salmon. I believe that Miss Megan Boyd did most of the work in popularising this pattern, and it is a particular favourite in Canada. There is a Canadian variation using a ruff of red ostrich herl on the head, and a further variation of winding fluorescent red floss over two-thirds of the head. Both of these ideas give the fly a sparkle of colour at the head and, in theory, an aiming point for the fish well forward to ensure better hooking. This is the sort of fly that catches the eye when in the flybox, is thus likely to be used, and is thus equally likely to catch a salmon!

The yellow floss body is livened up with an oval silver rib, the hackle is dyed blue cock, and the black hair-wing can be either black or dark brown hair of any suitable consistency. In the illustration I have used dyed squirrel-tail. The original recipe calls for jungle-cock cheeks, but I have missed these out on the simplified Drury treble dressing, and on the tube-fly version.

Most people would fish this pattern on a double hook, in the low-water conditions of high summer.

Fig. 7

Traditional dressing (top left):
Simplified Drury treble (top right):
Tube fly (bottom)

BLACK PENNELL

Fig. 8

Original pattern (top left): Drury treble (top right):
Tube fly – Mackenzie-Philps version (centre):
Small treble – Sean O'Brien version (bottom left):
Small single (bottom right)

BLACK PENNELL

H. Cholmondeley-Pennell was an inventive angler. Not only did he invent worming tackle, a range of hooks, several fly patterns, but he also wrote many books on fishing and the study of fish. He seems to have been most active between 1870 and 1886.

Perhaps the most durable of his fly patterns is the Black Pennell. Beloved of the trout and sea-trout angler, this pattern has caught a lot of salmon too, most of them by a happy accident while sea-trouting (original pattern top left).

For the Drury treble-hooked version I am indebted to Sean O'Brien. A superb angler and caster, Sean first told me of the dodge of dyeing G. P. tippet in hot orange dye to increase the impact of the tippet tail. He also suggests doing a whip finish before applying the heron hackle, so that this fragile component can be replaced without disturbing the body. The smaller treble is also his dressing, and is a variation on the Black Pennell theme, with a body of half-orange and half-black seal's fur (not unlike an Akroyd). Sean stresses that the tippet tail should be thick and bushy, to give a better appearance when viewed from the rear by the fish.

The small, single hook is another slight progression along this same theme, with a wing of unbleached squirrel-tail dyed orange, and then cut off square, to give points of orange light at the rear of the wing. The original of this pattern was found in the flybox of another superb Northern Ireland angler, Tommy McCutcheon, dresser unknown, and he and Sean developed this variation between them.

The tube fly is my own idea. Why not a Black Pennell on a tube? I tried using tippets at the rear but they did not please me. I find the appearance of the bleached and dyed orange squirrel-tail more to my liking and, when it suits them, to that of the salmon.

BLUE CHARM

In eighth place in 1983, and in thirteenth place in 1987, is the Blue Charm. We cannot tell if the 1987 figures include hair-wing versions, but I am certain that they do.

The original dressing, shown on the single hook, has two materials in the tag, a butt of ostrich herl and a topping over the wing. The wing is bronze mallard with a strip of teal. Nothing so complicated is required today, and the tube fly shows how simple the pattern can be and still be called a Blue Charm.

I have to thank D. & G. Flydressers of Aberdeen for the small tube. They call this a Parker tube fly, and it is dressed on a lightweight, flexible plastic tube, intended for low-water conditions. Lt Col Esmond Drury kindly provided the Drury treble version, which has yellow hair as a tail, has the extra glint of colour provided by the tag, and is a sleek-looking little fly. Malcolm Johnson of Knaresborough, a good angler and thoughtful fly-dresser, made the flexible lure using braided flyline backing Superglued to the shank and to the trailing treble: the ultimate answer to losing fish on rigid mounts.

Last, Fulling Mill Flies provided the double-hooked fly, which they call the Charming Blue. It is a Blue Charm with the addition of some strands of Lureflash Twinkle over the wing for an attractive extra sparkle.

BLUE CHARM

Fig. 9

Original pattern (top left):
Drury treble version (top centre): Parker tube fly (top right):
Simplified tube version (centre left): Charming Blue (centre right):
Trailing treble – Malcolm Johnson version (bottom)

BROOK'S SUNRAY FLY

Fig. 10

*Brook's Sunray Fly (top): Black and Red Pearl (centre):
Collie Dog (bottom)*

BROOK'S SUNRAY FLY

Invented for fishing fast water in Norway, the Brook's Sunray fly is the top fly in the illustration. Intended to be fished as a riffler, skating on the surface, the dressing incorporates long black hair, some slightly shorter brown hair, and a couple of strands of peacock herl, all lashed to a lightweight plastic tube. A good friend of mine who fishes regularly in Norway tells me that he has had salmon come across white water to smash into the fly, and that it seems to work best in bright weather. This fly is very similar to Hugh Falkus's Surface Riffler.

The centre fly is provided by Fulling Mill Flies, and is called a Black and Red Pearl. The total length is 18 cm (7 in)! Dressed on a plastic tube, the body is pearl Mylar tubing, ribbed with a scarlet cock hackle. The wing is held down by the turns of hackle, giving almost a Matuka effect and, like the Brook's Sunray, there are some peacock fibres in the wing. In addition there are some strands of pearl Lureflash on top of the wing, and a jungle-cock eye.

The third fly is the standard Collie Dog, dressed on an Esmond Drury treble. The silver body gives it a little glint at the head.

All of the above patterns are worth trying in hot weather, low-water, and apparently hopeless conditions. Find a spot at the head of a pool and dibble the fly across the surface, snaking it back and forth to leave a wake. You can sit on a rock and sunbathe at the same time!

CINNAMON SHRIMP

If you study the description and sketches of the food of salmon in the North Atlantic, you will become aware that some of the shrimps have certain features not found in any salmon fly.

The photograph is intended to give you some ideas when next you are sitting at your fly-tying vice: a general cinnamon or tobacco colour; a flash of gold to liven up the body; and a long tail to resemble the feelers of a shrimp (in the examples the black-tipped hair is fox-tail hair). Perhaps there should be a glint of colour in the feelers by adding a golden pheasant topping to the hair. The wing of fox-tail hair can be tied in, and the waste ends drawn down and back to form a beard hackle. Or the wing can be tied down at the rear of the body to form a shell-back effect. A ribbing on the body of fluorescent, red floss can resemble the luminous, red spots found on all the euphausiids.

If you believe the thesis that salmon think they are feeding when they take a fly, you can have great fun inventing your own shrimp-like fly to fool them with, using the picture merely as a source of ideas. Single hooks have been used for ease of photography – I would use Esmond Drury trebles for my fishing flies.

CINNAMON SHRIMP

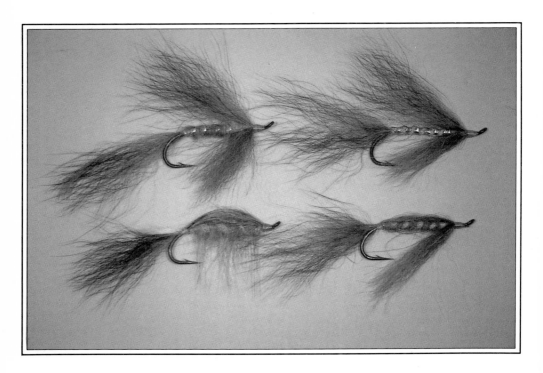

Fig. 11

Four examples of shrimp-based patterns using fox-tail hair.

COPYDEX FLY

Fig. 12

Copydex fly – Ken Fairclough version (top):
Treble – Peter Mackenzie–Philps version (2nd from top):
Double – Ken Fairclough version (3rd from top):
Treble – Peter Mackenzie–Philps version (bottom)

COPYDEX FLY

For this interesting idea I am indebted to a nice man – retired, disabled angler Ken Fairclough, of Aspull near Wigan. He had the idea of trying latex bodies for salmon flies, and two of the illustrated flies, the top one and the third one, are his originals on which he has caught fish. The second and fourth ones are my experiments to test the ease of manufacture.

The fly is dressed in two parts. First, the hook or mount is prepared using seal fur, squirrel-tail hair, palmered hackle, or whatever. The body is then attached using copper wire. The body is made by painting Copydex adhesive onto a sheet of glass, allowing to dry until tacky (I left it for twenty-four hours), and then rolling the Copydex up into a sausage-shaped body. If lines are drawn with a felt pen on the Copydex before rolling, a striped effect is obtained. The Copydex can be rolled around a strand of wool to give a coloured glow through the body and a tuft at each end.

While the fly looks like some form of hairy worm, it does work extremely well, and Ken has had some great sport on the Tay, Lune, and Nith, and on Loch Ba, using a sinking line to get the fly down deep. In strong currents he sometimes adds a small swivel and bomb weight a metre or so up the leader, but this can then only be fished by harling – the bomb and fly together make an uncastable combination for a fly rod.

On the occasions that these flies have been used, they have outfished conventional flies and spinners. But what do the salmon take them for?

CROE FOX

Invented by Mr John (Jackie) Macrae, of Inverinate, for fishing his local river, the Croe. Although the Croe is a short, West-Highland spate river, the fly has been used very successfully on other rivers. Fishing the Croe one day, Mr Macrae was seen by a man who had just shot a fox attacking his lambs, and was given the tail. From that came these flies.

Fox-tail hair, from the upper surface, is a very soft hair, grey at the roots, gingery in the centre, and with black tips. The hair from the underside of the tail does not have the black tips. The dressing as given to me by Mr Macrae is a yellow tying-thread body with a silver rib, with a wing of fox hair, reddish with black tips, and tied long. The red head is found to be attractive to cock salmon at the back-end of the season – aggression triggered by the red? In the illustrations I have not used red varnish, but an overlay of fluorescent red floss before using clear varnish. Mr Macrae tells me that he uses hooks size 4 to 12, singles, doubles, trebles, or tubes, depending upon the conditions.

In the illustration, the top two flies are dressed to the original recipe, as is the tube. On the bottom row are a couple of variations, both with a gold body to add a glint, and a jungle-cock eye to smarten up the appearance a little. The fly on the left is dressed, not with fox-tail hair, but with partly-bleached grey squirrel tail hair. Dipped in a 30–30–30 mixture of peroxide, ammonia, and hot water, grey-squirrel tails will easily attain this gingery colour in a few minutes.

CROE FOX

Fig. 13

Original pattern (top left):
Original pattern treble (top right): Tube-fly version (centre):
Grey squirrel versions (bottom row)

DUNKELD

Fig. 14

Traditional version (top left):
Squirrel and Orange (top right): Tube-fly version (centre):
Malcolm Johnson variation (bottom left):
Simplified dressing – on Drury treble (bottom right)

DUNKELD

Long a favourite fly of the trout angler on lochs, the sea-trout angler and, in an enlarged version, for salmon, this Scottish pattern could best be described as a Thunder and Lightning but with an all-gold body instead of the black floss and oval gold ribbing.

The traditional dressing for salmon has a tag of yellow or gold floss, and a butt of ostrich herl, but apart from those, the fly at the top left is near enough. Next to it at the top is an even more simple version, with a grey-squirrel tail hair-wing instead of the mallard bronze, which should properly be called a Squirrel and Orange.

The tube-fly version has been dressed using orange and brown bucktail, and in common with the traditional pattern it should really have a hackle of blue jay instead of the dyed guineafowl.

At the bottom left is a pattern tied by Malcolm Johnson of Knaresborough. The body is silver, but the combination of colours gives the impression of a Dunkeld with an added sparkle because of the number of colours of hair in the wing. Bottom right is the simplified Dunkeld dressed on an Esmond Drury treble, and is the fly I would choose to fish with instead of the traditional dressing nowadays. All the three colours on this fly – orange, brown, and blue – are bleached and dyed squirrel-hair.

Why a hair-wing version? Ask any fly-dresser and he will tell you that mallard bronze feathers are perhaps the most difficult material apart from teal with which to obtain a neat wing, yet the colour is apparently attractive to fish.

ELIZABETH OF GLAMIS

In 1980, Her Majesty the Queen Mother was eighty years old. This country's most-loved salmon angler, she had never had a fly named after her, and my wife, Sue, and I decided that it was time that this omission was rectified. The fly we tied works especially well for clear water in the summer. The colouring of the fly was dictated for us. When we thought of the Queen Mother, we visualised her with silver hair, dressed in pastel colours, pearl-grey and pink seeming to be favourites at that time, and we added a touch of gold to give the fly a regal appearance!

The dressing, therefore, was as follows:

Tag: Fluorescent, pink floss. To make this show better, the hook was first painted with Tipp-Ex – Peter calls this his typing-mistake paint!

Body: Pearl-grey or pale-blue dun wool, seal's fur, or man-made fibre, with a silver rib – three touching turns before an open spiral up the body.

Tail and topping: Golden pheasant crest.

Hackle: Cock hackle, or bleached and dyed squirrel-tail, fluorescent pink.

Wing: Squirrel tail, bleached and dyed pale-blue dun or pearl-grey, with a jungle-cock eye. Head black, varnished several coats to appear glossy.

The fly on the left is one of the 1980 originals, dressed on a single hook so that the appearance can be better assessed. The fly on the right is how I dress it nowadays for fishing, on an Esmond Drury treble, and with a simplified dressing.

The fly has caught me fish in both bright and dull conditions. I have never dressed it as a tube fly as the appearance on a tube does not appeal to me.

Fig. 15

Original dressing (left):
Simplified version – on Drury treble (right)

FALKLANDS FLASHER

Fig. 16

Original pattern (top left):
Double hooked version (top right): Tube-fly version (centre):
Lureflash – on Drury treble (bottom left and right)

FALKLANDS FLASHER

In 1982 the Falklands were invaded, and British forces showed their professionalism and standards of training and dedication at a cost of two hundred and fifty lives. Shortly after the war was over, work started on a new airport and one of our customers, a keen angler, went out to work on the project. His letters told us of sea-trout fishing of a magical standard. Most fish were put back, but those of 4.5 kg (10 lb) were not rare. We sent him some of the then-new, flashy, man-made materials, and he reported that a simple fly, made of Lureflash alone, was the most effective sea-trout fly in the rivers of the Falklands.

The fly at the top left is one of his originals. Tie in a bunch of Lureflash as a tail, wind the rest up the shank to form the body, and lash the remainder back as a wing – all done with one length of Lureflash, and the total time to dress a fly is less than a minute. This one has the barb of the hook flattened so that fish can be returned with as little damage as possible. It is very similar in construction to the Yorkshire Flasher, which was made of mosaic Lureflash, a darker multicolour. Top right is a double-hooked version, but with pearl Mylar tubing for the body, and a jungle-cock eye to spruce it up a little. This fly has caught two salmon, so is looking a little tired.

The tube fly in the centre has also caught a couple of salmon, and is also dressed with pearl Mylar tubing and pearl Lureflash.

Below are two suggestions for simple flies, using Esmond Drury trebles, Lureflash, and copper wire to give a simple, squid shape with a glitter to catch the eye. Although I mention Lureflash, Flashabou is almost the same material and can be substituted – you would be hard put to tell the difference.

FLEXIFLIES

Flexiflies are tube flies, dressed on brass or copper tubes, with a rubber tube at the rear to take the eye of the treble hook. Always dressed with Mylar braided tubing for a glittery body, the colour can vary as seen in the illustration.

The size of the silver treble should be noted, as this is the suggested size for reliable hooking. Compare this with the size of the black treble below – the size chosen by many anglers who then complain that many fish hooked on tube flies 'just come unstuck'.

The black and silver fly with the small, black treble is dressed on a lightweight plastic tube that has a socket moulded at the rear.

The yellow and orange fly could be called a Garry Dog with a gold body instead of the black floss and gold rib normal on this pattern. This is a good fly for coloured water. The black and yellow could be called a Tosh, the black and red an Oglebug. For further tube flies, see Various Tube Flies, page 179. 'Flexifly' is a trade mark of Esmond Drury (Salmon Flies) Ltd.

FLEXIFLIES

Fig. 17

Tube flies – all dressed with Mylar braided tubing.
Note size of hook on first fly (this is correct size)

GARRY DOG

Fig. 18

Modern pattern (top left):
Esmond Drury Garry Dog (top centre): Parker tube fly (top right):
Modern tube-fly version (centre left): John's Shrimp (centre right):
Garry Glitter (bottom)

GARRY DOG

Invented by John Wright, the son of the famous James Wright of Sprouston, this fly is the subject of much confusion. Originally dressed with a wing of hair from a golden retriever called Garry, the yellow and red mixture is nowadays supposed to represent the sandy-gold colour of the original. The fly is also known as a Garry, or Yellow Dog.

The fly at the top left is the accepted modern pattern, dressed on a single hook for clarity. Next to it on the top row is an Esmond Drury Garry Dog, and at the right is a Parker tube fly as sold by D. & G. Flydressers of Aberdeen, in a size suitable for low water.

In the centre left is the modern tube fly as dressed for use in coloured water, or in spring or autumn. Some fly-dressers mix the hair before tying it in, and some layer the colours as is done here. With a body of copper Lurex, this fly becomes a Copper King.

Centre right the fly is a shrimp pattern invented by an excellent angler, John Green of Halifax. He mixes yellow, red, and orange hair in the wing, and the body is flat, gold tinsel. Dressed long on an Esmond Drury treble, the fly is an excellent one in coloured water. His friends call the fly 'John's Shrimp', but it can be regarded as a Garry Dog with a gold body, jungle-cock cheeks, and a red head.

Equal bunches of yellow, red, and blue hair around the shank, and the fly becomes a Pilkington.

Below is a further variation. Called a Garry Glitter, Fulling Mill Flies use Lureflash in addition to the hair in the wing for extra sparkle.

Add some black hair to the wing mixture of a Garry Dog tube fly, and the fly becomes a Willie Gunn!

HAIRY MARY

Dressed originally by John Reidpath of Inverness as a hair-wing version of the Blue Charm, the Hairy Mary has a gold rib instead of the silver ribbing of the Charm. The original brown hair was fitch tail or bucktail.

In the top left, I have dressed a Hairy Mary near to the original dressing. Nowadays the usual commercial offering has a wing of grey squirrel (top right).

The tube fly in the centre uses the same hair as top left – bleached and dyed squirrel-tail from a grey squirrel shot in the winter – quite long hair can be found on a winter tail. For larger tubes it would be necessary to use bucktail or similar longer hair. Fox-squirrel tail is an alternative.

Bottom left is the Esmond Drury commercial offering, and it is interesting to see that the blue hackle is applied underneath the grey squirrel wing. Bottom right is the Parker tube as sold by D. & G. Flydressers of Aberdeen, suitable for low-water conditions, and very light in weight.

An excellent fly, the Hairy Mary took over from the Blue Charm in the survey of flies from the *Trout and Salmon* magazine river reports (see Chapter 3).

HAIRY MARY

Fig. 19

Traditional Dressing (top left): Modern version (top right):
Tube-fly version (centre):
Esmond Drury Hairy Mary (bottom left):
Parker tube version (bottom right)

LADY CAROLINE

Fig. 20

Heron-hackle version (top left):
Blue Dun cock-hackle version (top right):
Lady Caroline treble (bottom)

LADY CAROLINE

Invented for fishing the Spey, the Lady Caroline has the typical Spey heron hackle and low-lying wing. The wings in the examples illustrated have been perked up a little deliberately to show the body details – normally they would lie so low as to hide the body when viewed from the side. The original dressing for the Lady Caroline suggested olive-green and light-brown Berlin wools twisted together, two of brown to one of olive-green. Nowadays it is acceptable to use a light, brown-olive seal's fur or similar fibre.

Heron is a feather the possession of which is illegal unless one can prove that it came into one's possession before the passing of the Wildlife and Countryside Act 1981. I can, and I have ten hackles left! The fly at top left is dressed using heron. A large, Blue Dun cock-hackle has been used top right, and a straggly beard of natural-brown bucktail fibres for the fly at the bottom. In all cases the tail is golden pheasant red-spear fibres, and the wing is mallard bronze. The original dressing called for two ribbings criss-cross, the second to hold the palmered hackle.

A most useful fly, suggesting a shrimp-like shape, subdued natural colouring, and if the hackles are mobile, a movement and suggestion of life. It must be emphasised that the wing should be low-slung over the body in Spey style, and this is best achieved by tying each wing on separately, reversing the thread in between, and aiming to anchor the wing roots at the side of the hook rather than on top.

LEADHEADS

Every fly seen by a salmon is travelling horizontally. Try a lead-head, and your fly will be the first fly the fish will have seen to be travelling up and down. Stillwater anglers often know these leadheaded flies as Dog Nobblers.

The top fly (fly?) is sold by Shakespeare for jiggling for sea fish, under the name of Porky Jig. Tied to a strong leader, and cast gently into the fast water at the head of a deep pool, the rod tip should then be slowly lowered and raised to give a tantalising action up and down in the water. I do stress that the movement should be slow – do it quickly and someone will accuse you of trying to snig a fish, and that is not the idea at all.

The fly below is lighter, dressed on a longshank lure-hook size 8, and has caught a salmon. The bushy marabou tail moves enticingly in the water, and this style can be dressed in any colour combination you fancy, on any kind of hook.

The weight at the head of the hook does not need to be made of split shot, pinched and Superglued in place. Just as effective is to wind a ball of lead wire around the shank, well varnished to hold it in place and, if you wish, you can camouflage it by winding a head of peacock herl over the top.

A simple idea, calculated to give apoplexy to the traditionalist, it does work in places where it is allowed by the rules of the beat.

LEADHEADS

Fig. 21

Shakespeare Porky Jig (top): Size 8 leadhead (bottom)

LORD LOUIS

Fig. 22

Lord Louis treble (top): Tube-fly version (bottom)

LORD LOUIS

Invented by the author in 1983, this fly was intended for fishing the Tweed, but has caught salmon in many Scottish rivers since. The basic idea was a white wing. This aspect has a reputation for being successful in the evening. The body is fluorescent magenta, as Tom Saville reckons that this is a useful colour when the sun is low. The black hackle at front and rear gave a slightly more solid silhouette, and the yellow centre hackle gave a small additional sparkle of colour to catch the eye. The colours turned out to be very similar to the colours of the campaign ribbon for the Burma Star, and so the fly was named in honour of Earl Mountbatten of Burma and called the Lord Louis.

I caught my first salmon on this fly at midday, in a glaring sun! I caught my second fish on it in the evening, about half an hour after sunset. Now I am not sure whether it should be regarded solely as an evening fly or not – all I am sure of is that it was *intended* to be an evening fly ... but when I am desperate I will try anything.

One of my friends ties a silver, oval ribbing on the body, claiming that the extra sparkle is useful at times, and while this may well be true, the original, and all the examples in my box, do not have a rib.

MARCH BROWN

Going back into the mists of time, this pattern has been a favourite of the salmon and trout angler for centuries. It has been referred to as the original shrimp pattern, although it is named after the up-winged fly that hatches on many northern and Scottish rivers in March and April.

It is dressed in the traditional manner at the top left, with the addition of a golden pheasant crest in the tail to give a little extra sparkle. The wings of a salmon version are best tied with hen-pheasant tail-feathers, although a trout-sized fly will be better dressed with hen-pheasant secondary wing-quills, as the tail fibres do not stay married well enough on smaller sizes.

The fly is often seen in the low-water style shown top right, where the same size of hook has been used (in this case, not a low-water style of hook, but the same hook), yet the fly gives a much smaller impression without losing the hooking ability of the larger hook.

Below is a variation, on an Esmond Drury treble, using grey squirrel tail fibres for the wing. Strands of partridge hackle could have been bearded just as well, but would have been a trifle fragile for a salmon fly, in my opinion.

The March Brown is a most useful fly to fish as a dropper, in sizes 8 to 10, and works well even in lochs where the fish can never have seen a living March Brown fly in their lives. If there is still fishing going on three centuries from now, I have no doubt that the March Brown will still be a favourite fly – if they can get the feathers and hare's fur!

MARCH BROWN

Fig. 23

Traditional dressing (top left): Low-water variant (top right):
Squirrel-tail version – on Drury treble (bottom)

MAR LODGE

Fig. 24

Simplified hair-wing version (top left):
Sparsely-dressed treble (top right): Tube-fly version (bottom)

MAR LODGE

An old pattern, originally fully dressed with a feather-mixed wing of bronze and grey mallard, plus coloured strips of dyed swan, the Mar Lodge originated for fishing the Dee.

In the hair-wing simplified version shown, the wing is grey squirrel as a base, with mixed yellow, blue, red, and brown hair on top. In the treble-hooked version I have mixed the wing fibres before tying them in, and deliberately dressed the fly sparsely, giving the impression I prefer.

The tube fly is dressed in a more bulky fashion, and the wing has been splayed out to show the body detail – normally I would dress a Mar Lodge tube to give a sleeker effect, but then body detail would not show on the photograph.

The fly is a difficult pattern to tie, as the body is in three parts, flat silver tinsel at each end, and black floss in the centre, with a silver oval rib overall. Mixing the fibres for the wing is also a fiddly business – blending little bunches of hair by rolling in the fingers. All the trouble is worth it if the end result has that sleek, shimmering appearance suggested by the dressing on the treble illustrated, and the fish find it attractive too.

MEGAN

Invented, I believe, by Miss Megan Boyd MBE, this fly is a favourite on the Brora and the Helmsdale in summer. Usually dressed on small, lightweight tubes, or doubles size 8 and 10, the normal dressing is as shown top left. It is a sombre-looking fly, but very effective.

I have to thank Colin Wilson of Horwich for details of his favourite fly, and it is shown at the top right – a variation of the Megan using blue-dyed squirrel-tail for the wing. The tips of the squirrel hair should be the same colour as the hackle and tail.

Next is shown the tube-fly version, where the blue hackle can be overlaid short, or be mixed in with the wing, or be dressed in alternate bunches of blue and black around the tube. The fish do not seem to mind. This tube fly is sometimes called a Bruiser, when the blue and black hairs are mixed in the wing.

Last, on the double hook is shown a fly dressed by Tom Saville of Nottingham. He calls it a Crathie, and he usually dresses it on a low-water double, size 8 to 12. Originally the hackle was polar-bear hair, but as supplies of this have dried up, he now uses good, shiny, cock hackles dyed light blue or fluorescent blue. Tom has stressed to me that the wing must lie sleekly low, and that the fly should be tied on Partridge low-water hooks, as these have just the correct shape for the impression the fly should give. The jungle-cock cheeks are an essential part of the pattern. An honest angler, Tom tells me that this fly catches 80 per cent of his fish perhaps because he uses it 80 per cent of the time! While this fly could be described as a silver-bodied Megan, it is fair that we credit Tom with the recipe and call it a Crathie.

MEGAN

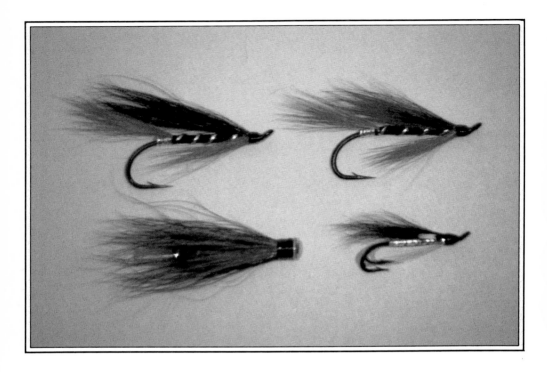

Fig. 25

Traditional dressing (top left): Colin Wilson variation (top right):
Bruiser (bottom left): Crathie – double hook (bottom right)

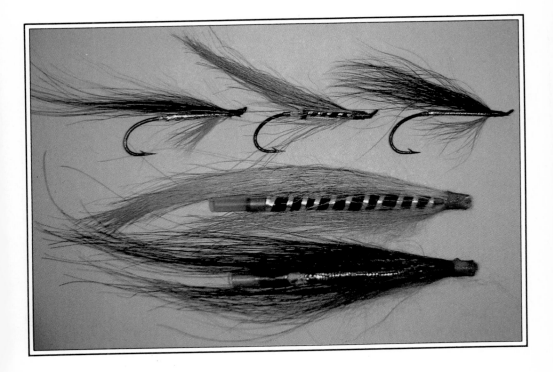

Fig. 26

*Millcraig Magenta (top left): Millcraig Gold (top centre):
Chamberlain (top right): Millcraig Gold tube fly (centre):
Chamberlain tube fly (bottom)*

MILLCRAIG

Invented by Arthur Chamberlain of Alness, the Millcraig flies are those he uses when he so often catches the first salmon of the season from his local rivers.

Top left is the Millcraig Magenta. Dressed with a long hair-wing, the magenta hackle gives a pleasant glow of colour and makes the fly very successful for grilse and summer salmon. Top centre is the Millcraig Gold. Again, the long hair-wing is a feature, and the colour is important. A very strong, dirty yellow is the original, but a colour close to it can be obtained by blending yellow and orange hair. The fly is successful in water that is fining off after a spate, but still with a touch of peat in it. Top right is a fly that caught the first salmon out of a new pool on the Alness (Averon) river a few years ago, and that was named the Chamberlain by Bill Topham, the river superintendent who does such a good job on this lovely river.

Below are tube-fly versions of the Millcraig Gold and the Chamberlain. The bottom tube produced a 9.8-kg (21½-lb) fish from the Tweed in November 1986, and the first fish out of the Helmsdale on 21 January 1987. It was generous of Arthur Chamberlain to dig these flies out of his box and send them to me for this book – they are fish-catching flies, not dressed specially for the photograph.

MUDDLER MINNOW

'Surely nobody but an English reservoir angler would go to Scotland and try to catch a salmon on a Muddler!' So ran the comment of an old Scottish friend of mine, an experienced salmon angler. I was able to assure him that all the flies in the illustration, or close copies of them, have caught salmon.

Top left is the original Muddler Minnow dressing, with a wing of oak turkey among the squirrel-tail hair, a gold body, and a collar left after barbering the plump head. It has proved to be a great fly for salmon in west-coast lochs and, used as a skating fly, one of my friends uses it in preference to any other salmon fly. Top right is a tandem badger Muddler, dressed on two size-6 lure hooks joined by 9 kg (20 lb) monofil. The silver bodies give a nice glint and the plump head is supposed to create a vibration in the water (but I personally doubt if it does). This fly has caught two summer salmon of about 4.5 kg (10 lb). It is basically a Conon Lure with a Muddler head added to it.

Bottom left is a tandem marabou Muddler, also dressed on two size-6 lure hooks, joined with monofil. Black deer-hair, black marabou, and this is a copy of the fly that caught three fish for a friend of mine on a day when no one else caught a thing. Fishing in the sea pool of a West-Highland spate river, he thought he might have a chance of a sea-trout, but he caught only salmon! Bottom right is a Muddler that has accounted for four salmon in one day. A day of baking heat, the river down to its bones, and the fly was fished on 2.75-kg (6-lb) nylon to salmon lying in the shade of a high bank and trees. I am told that fish that had been in the river for two weeks came up through 3.7 m (12 ft) of water to take it. Looks like a little squid? I wonder. But Muddlers catch salmon.

Fig. 27

*Traditional dressing (top left): Tandem badger Muddler (top right):
Tandem marabou Muddler (bottom left): Muddler – 'squid' (bottom right)*

Fig. 28

Traditional dressing (top left): Esmond Drury dressing (top right):
Mackenzie-Philps dressing (bottom left): Commercial variation (bottom right)

MUNRO KILLER

Major John Ashley-Cooper, fishing one day on the lovely Knockando beat of the Spey, wanted a Thunder and Lightning. He had no mallard bronze feathers in his kit, so he used hair from a yellow-dyed squirrel-tail instead. He had a wonderful afternoon, catching several salmon, and talked that night in the bar of the Dowans Hotel. Other guests, wanting a similar fly, hurried to Mr Munro – the Aberlour tackle-dealer and fly-dresser – and described the pattern. The news spread like wildfire along the Spey valley. The originator was forgotten, but the man who copied the fly was remembered. Thus was born the fly that occupies third place in our table of Scottish patterns in Chapter 3. It is a good general-purpose fly for dull weather.

Top left is a copy of the original pattern – black-floss body with an oval gold tag and ribbing. The front half of the body has a palmered orange cock hackle, and there is then a beard of blue jay. The wing is yellow-dyed squirrel tail. Top right is one of Colonel Esmond Drury's commercial flies. The dressing is very similar – not surprising, as he was a personal friend of John Ashley-Cooper. The only difference is that the orange hackle is bearded and, because jay fibres are very short, blue-dyed guineafowl has been used instead.

Bottom left is a variation as sold by Mackenzie-Philps Ltd, of Wetherby, dressed by John Harris, where a black wing is used. Bottom right is a fly bought by the author in a Scottish tackle shop when he asked for a Munro's Killer. Nowadays this two-colour wing is a common variation, and still catches fish.

This fly is usually dressed on doubles or trebles. I have never seen a tube version.

Although originally called a Munro's Killer, it is today known as a Munro Killer.

PHEASANT TAIL NYMPH

Two good anglers, Les Holroyd from Goole and Alan Dawson from Nottingham, were fishing the Kirkholme beat of the Stinchar in October 1987. The weather was hot and bright, and the river was low – conditions most salmon anglers thought were impossible. They decided that unusual tactics were called for.

Alan started by trying a white Dog Nobbler, hooked one fish and lost it when the hook straightened out. He then tried a Pheasant Tail Nymph and, over the next two days, they had five fish each, and lost several when the hook straightened out. They eventually took it in turns to fish with their one remaining nymph, and had to keep re-setting the hook each time it straightened in a fish. (If ever there was a case for not economising on hooks, this was it!) On the second day they lent the nymph to another angler who was totally frustrated by his lack of success, and he hooked a fish and lost it when the hook straightened.

It is worth giving the dressing of the original fly: hook, longshank size 6 single; tail, pheasant-tail fibres; body, a mixture of red, olive, and light-ginger seal's fur to give an overall colour effect of cigarette tobacco, ribbed with copper wire; thorax, a thicker dubbing of the same seal's fur mixture; and wing case, pheasant-tail fibres, tied in to point backwards, brought over to form wing cases, and then doubled down and back to form legs.

Top left can be seen a copy of the original dressing, with a slightly darker version top right, and another dressed on an Esmond Drury treble with a longer tail. It even looks like a shrimp! (The singles are size 6, and the treble is a 4.) Fished in the shade of trees, twitched like a wet fly, this fly produced salmon for two enterprising anglers when most other anglers had given up and gone home to sunbathe.

PHEASANT TAIL NYMPH

Fig. 29

Original dressing (top left): Dark pheasant tail (top right):
Drury treble version – long tailed (bottom)

POT SCRUBBER

Fig. 30

Original pattern (top left):
Simplified version on Drury treble (top right):
Coppery Pot Scrubber (centre left):
Simplified on nickel-plated hook (centre right):
Tube fly – with orange collar hackle (bottom)

POT SCRUBBER

Invented by John Mackenzie, the Pot Scrubber derives its name from the copper pan-scouring pad from which the original copper tinsel was extracted. Copper-coloured spinning baits are deservedly popular with anglers because they prove popular with the salmon. It seemed logical that a copper-coloured fly should be tried, and it has worked most successfully in clear and in coloured water.

Top left is the original pattern, but the body is copper Lureflash instead of tinsel. It works just as well. Next is a slightly simplified version on an Esmond Drury treble.

Below that, centre right, is a smaller nickel-plated hook with the same simplified version, to show the extra glint that can be obtained by using silvery hooks. Centre left is a more coppery effect. The Lureflash was wound along the body, and the waste ends drawn back to form an under wing after the ribbing has been brought up.

Below is a tube-fly version, with the addition of an orange collar hackle to give some extra colour for dirty water. The fly just looked a bit drab without it, and I sat and looked at it in the vice for several minutes before deciding upon the addition of the orange. This version has not been fished with, unless somebody else has devised it unbeknown to me.

PRAWN FLIES

Ever since anglers realised that salmon fed on prawns in the ocean they have been trying to dress flies to resemble this crustacean. And they catch fish very well.

Top left is an original Esmond Drury fly, the General Practitioner, which he invented so many years ago, and which has become a standard salmon pattern. Top right is a fly I was sold in a Scottish tackle shop as a General Practitioner, and it has caught me a salmon.

Centre left is a fluorescent-pink prawn fly as sold by James Waltham of Warrington, and it is interesting to note that the fly is dressed first, and dyed second! Centre right is a latex-bodied prawn fly as sold by Fulling Mill Flies. The eyes are made of monofil, melted into blobs at the ends using a candle flame.

The two bottom flies are prawn flies as sold by Steve Parton of Sparton Fishing Tackle. Steve tells me that some of his customers fish these flies under a float when they are not allowed to use the real thing – does the addition of a float mean that they are no longer fly fishing? While I grin at the thought, they are using fly-fishing tackle with a fly on the end – why should the float make a difference?

All of these flies will catch salmon, but I still wonder if the salmon *think* they are eating a prawn when they take one. Lay the wing of a Durham Ranger on its side and you have a General Practitioner – do the salmon think a Durham Ranger is a prawn?

PRAWN FLIES

Fig. 31

General Practitioner – original Drury dressing (top left):
'General Practitioner' – commercial dressing (top right):
Fluorescent-pink prawn fly (centre left):
Latex-bodied prawn fly (centre right):
Steve Parton prawn flies (bottom left and right)

PURPLE McBAIN

Fig. 32

Traditional dressing (top):
Tube-fly version, with buck-tail wing (bottom)

PURPLE McBAIN

There are very few salmon flies around that have purple in them — one or two prawn and shrimp patterns, but few tradional flies. The Purple McBain is a fly invented by Mr Gordon McBain, of Aberdeenshire, and the flies above were dressed by D. & G. Fly Dressers of Aberdeen.

This pattern has accounted for forty-nine salmon in seven rivers over a period of four years, so it must be regarded as a successful pattern. Dressed on tubes from 13 mm (½ in) to 5 cm (2 in) long, or on singles, doubles, or trebles from sizes 4 to 10, the fly works all year round, the size only being varied to suit the conditions.

The tube fly pictured has a wing of bucktail. The fineness of the hair is unusual for bucktail, and Mr Forbes, of D. & G., tells me that he uses only the tips of the hair in order to achieve this fineness. By avoiding the roots of the hairs, it will be found that bucktail can be tied in to lie sleekly on a tube rather than flaring out too much, as will happen when the thick, hollow butt ends of the hairs are compressed by the tying silk.

Why on earth is purple such an effective colour for a salmon bait? Prawn fishers go to great lengths to obtain dyed prawns of just the correct purple, so there must be something to be said for the colour. Mr McBain's forty-nine salmon tend to suggest that the colour works on a fly too.

ROGIE

Bill Brown of Strathpeffer, known as Rogie, writes river reports for *Trout and Salmon* magazine, covering much of the north of Scotland. He has been a dedicated salmon angler for many years and has developed an intelligence network over a wide area. Many years ago he fished the Conon regularly, and the ghillie on the Brahan beat dressed a fly for him, using the then-new Lurex materials. The colour they chose together was red, and so the Black Brahan fly was born: a long tail of black squirrel-tail hair, a red Lurex or Lureflash body with a silver oval ribbing, and a long wing, also of black squirrel. This fly is shown on the large treble in the photograph.

Around 1980, Rogie was talking to Bill Topham, the river superintendent of the Alness, who lives at Novar. They decided that a different fly was needed for the conditions that day, and Rogie suggested a body of green Lurex. Bill dressed the fly, shown in the photograph in tube and small, double-hooked styles, and it has caught fish at all times of the season in many rivers in the north of Scotland. Bill christened it the Rogie. The dressing is a green Lurex body with a silver ribbing, and a mixed wing of yellow, orange, and black dyed hair.

Both the Rogie and the Black Brahan can be dressed in any size from 8-cm (3-in) tubes down to size 12 doubles and trebles. They were perhaps the first recognised patterns to use coloured tinsel bodies for that extra little sparkle that catches the eye of a salmon. Both patterns seem to work best when fished fast. Coloured Lurex in widths suitable for tube flies is not easy to find. It will be found that a bunch of strands of Lureflash can be wound to give a similar effect.

Fig. 33

Tube-fly version (top):
Rogie double-hook (bottom left):
Black Brahan treble (bottom right)

SHEEP SERIES

Fig. 34

Black Sheep double (top left): Red Sheep double (top right): Silver Sheep double (bottom)

SHEEP SERIES

For those fly-dressers who are alarmed at the imminent demise of seal's fur for bodies, there is hope. Sheep's wool, chopped into short lengths, can be an excellent substitute. (And cut short enough, can be just as difficult to dub!) The Sheep series of flies was introduced by Colonel J. Bates of America for fishing on the east coast of the United States and Canada for Atlantic salmon, and the flies in the photograph were provided for me by Jimmy and Joyce Robinson, fly-dressers of Alnwick, Northumberland.

The fly top left is the Black Sheep. The dressing is a black-dyed sheep's wool body with a silver tag and ribbing, light-blue hackle, and a wing of black bucktail with yellow over. The jungle-cock eye is tied in long, and the head must be red. Top right is the Red Sheep: same body, ribbing, and hackle, jungle-cock eye, and red head, but the wing is black, red, and black bucktail layered one after the other. Below is the Silver Sheep, dressed like the Black Sheep except for the all-silver body.

These flies are usually dressed on singles and doubles, in sizes 4 to 10. Trebles can be used in the UK, but are illegal in most of the United States and Canada, and frowned upon in some places in Scandinavia. Not, I would hasten to add, that there is anything unsporting about trebles as such, but some people put them to nefarious use and the law-abiding had to suffer along with the criminals.

SHRIMP FLIES

Put simply, one can 'shrimp' any pattern by putting a centre hackle on the body and leaving the tail long, but shrimp flies have evolved over the last century. On the Usk and the Wye, in the late 1800s, the grub flies were palmered. Nowadays the Usk Grub is a shrimp pattern, with three hackles.

Starting top left, there is a commercial shrimp fly I bought some years ago in a Scottish tackle shop. Notice how the tail is not a wound hackle as is usual, but is composed of two complete breast feathers from a golden pheasant. The rear part of the body dominates the pattern, the front part of black floss being hardly seen. With orange floss on the rear part, and an orange centre hackle, this would be an Usk Grub as is recognised today. Top right is the Esmond Drury commercial shrimp pattern, neatly dressed with a wound tail hackle.

Bottom left, dressed on a single for clarity of photography, is Curry's Red Shrimp, invented by Pat Curry of Coleraine. Omitted are the small red cheeks of Indian crow suggested in the original dressing. Bottom right is an orange and gold shrimp pattern as sold by Mackenzie-Philps Ltd before the business was sold in 1986. It looks a little tired as it has caught a salmon and has lain in my flybox for several years! The wing is bleached and dyed squirrel tail, three orange hackles, a flat gold tinsel body, and red head. A good fly on a bright day. Do the salmon really think these flies are shrimps?

SHRIMP FLIES

Fig. 35

*Commercial dressing (top left): Esmond Drury dressing (top right):
Curry's Red Shrimp (bottom left): Mackenzie-Philps dressing (bottom right)*

SILVER BLUE

Fig. 36

Traditional dressing (top left):
Traditional dressing on double (top right)
Alexander Martin Waddington version (centre):
Drury treble – with teal (bottom left):
Treble with squirrel tail (bottom right)

SILVER BLUE

I can still see that salmon rising like a great trout up through 3 m (10 ft) of water to take my fly. I was so astonished that I did nothing until it was back at the bottom, and when I tightened it was well hooked. It was my first salmon, and I was about seventeen at the time. Needless to say, the fly – a Silver Blue – has been one of my favourites ever since. Also called a Teal, Blue and Silver, or Teal and Silver, this fly goes back at least one hundred and fifty years, and is a favourite for loch fishing for brown trout, for sea-trout, and for salmon. Is it taken as a little fish? The trout and sea-trout version is usually dressed with a tippet tail. Leave the tail off, paint the hook shank silver instead of using tinsel, and add a red head, and you have Hugh Falkus's Medicine Fly.

Top left is the traditional dressing. Top right is a small, double-hook version, so useful in high summer and low water.

In the centre is an original Alexander Martin Waddington, bought from the Glasgow shop in the early 1950s.

Bottom left is a Drury treble, with a Silver Blue dressed around the hook. It will be noticed that teal fibres that lie straight are hard to find. Bottom right is another treble hook, with grey squirrel tail substituted for the teal fibres – it gives a similar effect in the water and is an acceptable alternative. When dressed on trebles, the wing should be sparse, to allow the silver to gleam through.

For a darker effect, the wing can be bronze mallard. For an even brighter effect, dress the fly on a nickel-plated hook.

SILVER STOAT

The first-ever Stoat's Tail fly was dressed, I believe, by John Parker, who tied a wisp of stoat-tail hair on to a piece of starling quill, making a little tube fly about 20 mm (¾ in) long. He was fishing the Park beat of the Dee at the time. Since then many variations of the fly have evolved. The Silver Stoat is one of them, where black hair is used for wing and hackle, and a silver body gives a sparkle to the whole dressing.

Top left is the by-now traditional dressing. Top right is the revised, 'tarted-up' version, and I can hear some people say that the addition of a topping tail and over wing, and a jungle-cock eye, makes all the difference to human acceptability! I wonder if the fish would notice the difference?

In the centre is a double-hooked fly called the Executioner, as tied by D. & G. Fly Dressers of Aberdeen. The little red spot gives an eye-catching aiming point.

Bottom left is the Silver Stoat as sold by Esmond Drury, where a tail has been added to complement the silver body. Bottom centre is a tube dressed by Iain D. Ogden of Banchory. It is interesting that he has used a stainless-steel tube to yield the body colour. Bottom right is a Stoat's Tail dressed on an Esmond Drury treble, nickel-plated version, size 12. Because of the colour, I have classed it as a Silver Stoat.

This is a favourite fly throughout Scotland, fished in all sizes from the huge down to size-14 trebles, usually in the summer, and usually in low water. A black fly on a bright day? It bends the rule but it catches lots of fish.

SILVER STOAT

Fig. 37

Traditional dressing (top left):
Revised dressing (top right): Executioner (centre):
Esmond Drury Silver Stoat (bottom left):
Iain Ogden version (bottom centre): Stoat's Tail – Drury treble (bottom right)

SQUID

Fig. 38

Mackenzie-Philps pattern (top):
Muppets – with trebles (centre and bottom)

SQUID

I can already hear the purists swearing! No, I do not claim that these are salmon flies for the purist fly fisher. They are, however, a reasonable representation of some of the things salmon ate in the sea, and they are no more artificial than chunks of metal called spoons, or lumps of wood or plastic called Devons . . .

Top is a creation I dreamt up one day when I was thinking about squid. Dressed on a brass tube, it starts with a thin strip of Etha-foam wrapped into a rotund shape, then an overlay of bucktail, tied in first at the head and then again at the end of the tube. The jungle-cock eye is a luxury. I have never fished with it, and it is included here merely as an idea for you to ponder. Intended to be fished on a sinking line and a short leader, the buoyancy of the Ethafoam would keep the fly off the bottom.

Below are two Muppets, lashed onto Esmond Drury trebles. These are sold for sea fishing, and are available in a wide range of colours. Jigged up and down, or trolled slowly, they are effective in the sea, so why should they not also catch a fish that was a sea-dweller until a couple of days or weeks ago? I know two anglers who have caught fish on these Muppets, but they have both asked me not to name them as their friends thought they were fly fishing at the time! The beats were not 'fly only', so why should they both feel guilty?

STINCHAR STOAT

Put an orange hackle on a Stoat's Tail and some people would call it a Thunder Stoat. I believe that the pattern was first used on the Stinchar – it is currently widely used there and thus I prefer the name Stinchar Stoat.

Top left, on a single, is the typical pattern. Next to it is the version dressed by an exceptionally good angler, John Green of Halifax, who insists upon a long, black wing and a prominent collar hackle. John sometimes adds a long, black tail to this dressing.

Centre left is the Dark Stinchar, sold commercially by Esmond Drury. Centre right is his Orange Tosh – very similar in effect.

On the bottom row is the Duke's Killer, basically a Stinchar Stoat but with a body of hot orange or fluorescent orange chenille. First dressed by His Grace, the Duke of Wellington, in September 1979 when he was fishing his water at Knockdolian, it was named by Esmond Drury who was also fishing there at the time. On the first day it was used, in the form of a 2-in (5-cm) Waddington (but it has since been used in a variety of sizes down to treble 8), the Duke hooked four fish, landed three of them, and noted in his diary that the other eight rods fishing that day had caught only two between them. Of such things are born legends about fly patterns. This is a successful fly, particularly in dirty water or water just clearing after a spate.

STINCHAR STOAT

Fig. 39

Traditional dressing (top left): John Green dressing (top right):
Esmond Drury Dark Stinchar (centre left):
Esmond Drury Orange Tosh (centre right):
Duke's Killer treble (bottom left):
Duke's Killer tube fly (bottom right)

STOAT'S TAIL

Fig. 40

'Traditional' dressing (top left):
Esmond Drury Stoat's Tail (top centre): Size 14 nickel-plated treble
(top right): Black Maria (centre left): Red Butt Glodhack double
(centre right): Red Stoat double (bottom left): Palmered treble (bottom right)

STOAT'S TAIL

In theory, the original Stoat's Tail was an all-black fly, dressed on a tube, but the pattern as shown top left has evolved over the years to be the correct modern dressing: sombre, all black, and only relieved by the silver ribbing. Next to it is the commercial treble as sold by Esmond Drury. Top right is the tiny version proving so popular on Highland rivers in high summer. This particular sample was given to me by an angler who fishes regularly on the Dionard. It is dressed on a nickel-plated treble, size 14.

Tie a blue-dyed hackle point on each side of the wing (where the jungle-cock eyes normally go) and a Stoat's Tail becomes a Sweep. The centre row shows two further variations – with the rear half of the body made of yellow floss, a Stoat's Tail becomes a Black Maria, shown centre left. Centre right is a double-hooked fly called a Red Butt Glodhack, sold by Fulling Mill Flies and dressed for the Norwegian market.

Bottom row left is a double-hooked fly with a red hackle, called a Red Stoat, and is dressed by D. & G. Fly Dressers of Aberdeen. Bottom right is a treble with a palmered black hackle, and black hair wing, and a body of multicoloured Lureflash tinsel, to give a deep flash of colour among the fuzzy black.

All these flies will catch salmon, but they are a far cry from the original wisp of stoat's-tail hair lashed to a piece of starling quill!

TRADITIONAL PATTERNS

Shown here are some of the traditional patterns, carrying names that are by now famous and that account for many salmon each year throughout the world. These flies are all from Esmond Drury, taken straight from his commercial range, and in most cases – because they are dressed on trebles – the dressing has had to be simplified. Also in most cases, I have had to remove a little of the dressing so that the body details will show up for photography.

Top row, left to right: Black and Gold, Green Highlander, Jeannie, Logie.

Centre row: Silver Doctor, Blue Squirrel, Yellow Squirrel, Sweep.

Bottom row: Tadpole, Tosh, Thunder and Lightning.

From the flies in the picture, one can choose light or dark, bright or dull, depending upon the conditions and human whim, to give confidence while flogging away for hour after hour. However, if you half-close your eyes to get the picture slightly out of focus, is there really much difference between them? Do you really think that the salmon can tell the difference? Does your eye not keep coming back to the fly at the bottom left because it is a size larger than the others? And thus might not size be more important to the fish than the fine details of the pattern?

Consider the following scenario. You have seen a fish turn beside your fly. You are fishing with a size-8 Tosh and hunt desperately in your flybox for a size-4 Tosh to offer. You haven't got one. Should you really feel less confidence when trying a size-4 Black and Gold, Tadpole, or Jeannie?

TRADITIONAL PATTERNS

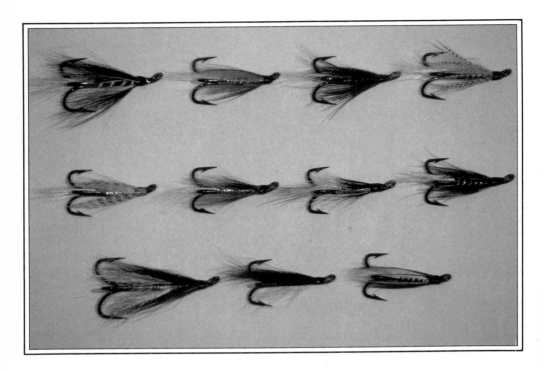

Fig. 41

Top row, left to right – Black and Gold, Green Highlander, Jeannie, Logie:
Centre row – Silver Doctor, Blue Squirrel, Yellow Squirrel, Sweep:
Bottom row – Tadpole, Tosh, Thunder and Lightning

VARIOUS TUBE FLIES

Fig. 42

Red Shrimp – D & G version (top left):
Lilac Time – Kenny Jack version (top right):
Gold Mylar tube fly (second row)
Gold Lureflash tube fly (third row, left): Belgian Flag (third row, right):
Confidence fly – Bill Topham's version (bottom left):
Pearl Mylar tube fly (bottom right)

VARIOUS TUBE FLIES

Tube flies can be of any pattern, colour, and brightness.

Top left is a Red Shrimp, as sold by D. & G. Fly Dressers of Aberdeen. Calling it a shrimp confuses, but many people tie something long on a tube and then call it a shrimp. Top right is Lilac Time, dressed by Kenny Jack, head boatman on Hendersyde. Kenny favours this successful fly for only the last hour of the day. He believes in a light-coloured fly as the light starts to go.

The very large fly is dressed with gold Mylar tubing, and has a wing of copper and red Lureflash tubing, with black bucktail over. Dressed on a 3-inch (8-cm) Supatube, the total length is 4 in (10 cm). You would used a spinner this length, why not a fly?

Third row left is a smaller version, but having gold Lureflash, and a small amount of orange and black bucktail over. Third row right is a Tweed fly, called a Belgian Flag. It has a three-part body and three sets of wings in black, yellow, and orange. Some anglers call this fly a Comet.

Bottom left is a Bill Topham Confidence fly. I was fishing the Alness one day with my son. After several hours we had caught nothing, then Bill appeared and suggested we try one of his Confidence flies. Ten minutes later I had a fish. Bill also gave a fly to my son, who had a fish. When we compared notes, the flies were totally different! Mine was the creation here; the other was light and bright. We christened this fly a Topham in happy memory of the occasion. Arthur Oglesby ties a very similar fly and his friends have christened it the Oglebug: an example of similar flies being known by different names, confusing anglers and the tackle trade but not the fish. Bottom right is a very light, bright fly, made of pearl Mylar tubing, silver Lureflash, and a white, brown, and orange bucktail.

The simplification of traditional patterns, in order to get them onto a tube, has been carried so far that many patterns are unrecognisable. There is a tendency to refer to tubes by their colours, for example, Black and Gold 3-in (8-cm) tube; and, while I regard this as unromantic, it helps identify the fly meant.

WILLIE GUNN

Rob Wilson of Brora tied up some tube flies one day, and laid them on the counter in front of Willie Gunn, a local ghillie. Willie chose the pattern that now bears his name, and which now accounts for 90 per cent of the flies sold from that famous shop. There are, however, already many variations.

Top row left is a fly dressed with equal quantities of black, yellow, and orange hair. A much darker effect is shown top right, where the amount of black hair is twice that of the other colours. Whichever effect you choose would depend upon the colour of the water, the colour of the sky, and your own personal hunch!

Centre left is the Esmond Drury commercial version, where the colours of hair have been tied on in succession. Centre right shows the different effect gained when the hair is mixed, or blended, before tying in. This is a fiddly job, but some might think it worth it for the sparkle of the blended colours.

Bottom left is a similar fly, called a Black Doctor by D. & G. Fly Dressers of Aberdeen – it has all the effect of a Willie Gunn, although red instead of orange has been used, and the colours are separated. Bottom right is another variant, called a Golden Gunn by Iain D. Ogden of Banchory. Dressed in any size from 13 mm (½ in) to 63 mm (2½ in), the fly has a yellow floss body, and is highly popular on the Deveron and Dee.

I have not shown this pattern on a single, as it was invented as a tube and is intended to have the hair blended all around the shank. There are all sorts of possibilities – Silver Gunn, Sporting Gunn (with a red waistcoat), Field Gunn (with a green body) – the mind boggles. But it is a great fish-catcher.

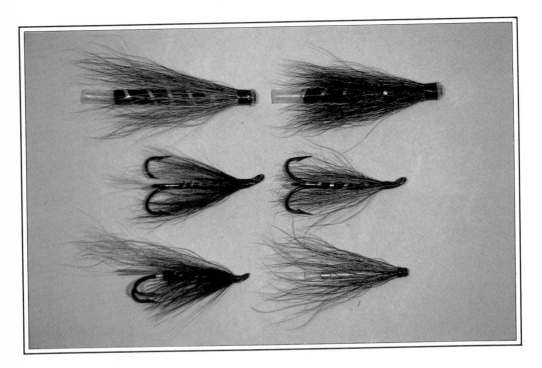

Fig. 43

Light version, tube fly (top left): Dark version, tube fly (top right):
Esmond Drury Willie Gunn (centre left):
Blended-hair variation (centre right):
Black Doctor – D & G version (bottom left):
Iain Ogden Golden Gunn (bottom right)

YELLOW TORRISH

Fig. 44

Traditional pattern (top left):
Orange Torrish (top right): Esmond Drury Yellow Torrish (centre left):
Parker tube fly – D & G version (centre right):
Silver Badger (bottom)

YELLOW TORRISH

Known as Torrish, Yellow Torrish, or Scalscraggie, this fly is not one of the all-time favourites but it is a reliable fish-catcher.

Top left is the modern, generally-accepted version, although I have omitted the butt of ostrich herl sometimes used. Some people use only yellow hair on the wing, but I feel that the fly loses much of its attractiveness if the teal is omitted. The top-left fly has a wing darker than I like, and a fortune awaits the person who discovers a hair that is marked in the fine, distinct speckle of a barred teal-feather! I do add a little yellow-dyed squirrel-hair under the teal wing. Change the hackle colour to orange, and you have an Orange Torrish, top right. Take a Yellow Torrish and change the wing to black hair, and you have a Kenny's Killer, not shown.

Centre left is the Esmond Drury commercial offering of the Yellow Torrish, and centre right is a Parker tube fly as tied by D. & G. Fly Dressers of Aberdeen. A variation of the Torrish is to have a yellow hair-wing and a blue hackle. The fly is then known as the Bourach, an excellent fly for bright conditions.

A similar fly to the Torrish family is shown at the bottom. Called a Silver Badger, it is dressed by Mayo Flycraft of Castlebar, Co. Mayo, and is the number-one fly for Lough Beltra and other Irish fisheries. Badger hair was used before the animal became protected, and grey squirrel is now substituted. A palmered yellow hackle and a blue beard give a family resemblance to the modern Yellow Torrish.

SWEETIE – A FLY FOR THE FUTURE?

In every angler there is an author bursting to get out. In every angler there is a new fly pattern longing to be invented. I am no different, and this book gives me the opportunity to display a new fly. I started by thinking of the shrimps I saw from the stomach contents of salmon, and I put together some of the common denominators of successful salmon flies.

I began with an Esmond Drury treble hook, and I tied in a long bunch of orange-dyed bucktail from the top of the tail, so the hair had brown roots – the feelers of the shrimp. Then comes a copper body with an oval silver ribbing, because I liked the look of it, and I wanted a glint but without the harsh appearance of flat silver or gold. The wing is a blended mixture of squirrel-tail dyed orange and yellow, with a few strands of teal over the top to give a slightly flecked appearance. A jungle-cock eye pleases my sense of tradition, and the whole fly is dressed with pale-olive tying-thread, varnished at the head with clear varnish. The wing should be dressed short, and the whole fly should look slim and sleek. The fly looks even more attractive when dressed on a nickel-plated treble, and I get all excited when I look at it and think of being able to try it out.

Why the name Sweetie? Two reasons: it is my nickname for my wife, Sue, and it reminds us of the small boy we overheard one day in Alness village who said to his mother in a lovely, soft, Highland accent, 'Mummy, I am in need of a wee sweetie'. We both fell about laughing. I am certain that the salmon will also feel that they are in need of a wee Sweetie when they see it.

SWEETIE

Fig. 45

Sweetie, shown enlarged.

APPENDIX
SUGGESTIONS ON THE
SIZE OF FLY

Nowhere in the text of this book have I mentioned the size of fly I recommend in differing conditions. There is a good reason for this. On several occasions I have caught a salmon at almost exactly the same time as another angler, on the same river, sometimes on the same beat. On one memorable day it happened within 36 m (40 yd) of the other man. Every single time this has happened, we have been using different-sized flies. Mine has been on a totally different size of hook from that used for the fly of the other man. It would be folly to infer that one of us was wrong in our choice of fly size – both flies caught fish.

I have never believed, therefore, in being dogmatic about the size of fly to use in any particular circumstance. There have been far too many examples of rules made by anglers that do not apply to the minds of salmon. Having said that, many anglers do want guidance and look for it from books or videos. They thirst for facts, advice, and suggestions, in an attempt to narrow the odds against not catching a fish. For this reason, for this reason alone, I thought it prudent to add some suggestions on the size of fly to choose from the box, in the hope that I might help to remove some of the agony of indecision that clings to most of us when we tackle up beside a salmon river. I cannot stress enough that anything I say from now on is only a *suggestion*. If I had believed all of it wholeheartedly, this would have appeared in the body of the book, and not as an appendix.

Let us start by saying that there does seem to be a correlation between water temperature and the size of fly likely to be successful. I have found it to be true that at water temperatures below about 6°C (42°F), a large tube fly is more likely to work than a small fly. Might this be because a large tube is usually fished on a sinking line, and is thus presented nearer to the nose of the fish – a fish that, because of the low temperature, is less inclined to travel far to take

Table 3 Temperature and hook size

Water Temperature		
°C	°F	Suggested hook size
Under 8	Under 45	Tube fly or 2
8–10	46–50	4
10–13	51–55	6
13–15	56–59	8
15–16	60–62	10
Over 16	Over 63	As small as you dare go

it? Perhaps. It therefore seems true that early-spring fishing is more likely to be successful if a large tube is used.

Some anglers assert that large tubes come into their own again in late autumn – not because of a drop in water temperature, but because the fish are more likely to feel aggressive to anything that threatens their redds or their sexual partners. Whether this is true or not, large tubes are frequently used for late-autumn fishing.

The agonies of indecision occur most frequently during the months that in Britain are laughingly called the summer months. I say this because I have felt chilled to the marrow in July and August in the north of Scotland and, at times, have taken water temperatures as low as 9°C (48°F) when there is some snow-melt going on in the hills. It is for the summer holiday angler that I repeat an old chart of temperatures and hook sizes I learned off by heart in my boyhood (see Table 3) and regarded as a firm rule (until I learned that it applied only when the salmon wanted it to!)

The suggested scale may be varied a little. It seems to be the case that shallow, fast-flowing water will cause a fly one size smaller to be acceptable. Equally, very fast-flowing water may well be the occasion to try a long tube fly instead of a standard hook pattern – witness the occasions when a Collie Dog will work in high summer and in water that feels like a bath. There are rivers where the rule seems a little adrift. I have heard it said that a smaller fly should always be used on the Aberdeenshire Dee than in other rivers, and this might just be caused by the fact that the Dee tends to be shallower than many other salmon rivers.

All I can suggest is that the speed of the current, the depth of the lie, and the temperature of the water should all be borne in mind

188

when choosing the size of fly to tie on the end of the leader. One day someone will produce a slide rule or computer programme that is based on pure logic and has these variables built in, and that will come up with an answer for the size of fly. And even when that day dawns it will be no more likely to be correct than a hunter's instinct or your pure hunch as you gaze at rows of flies and pick one out!

Hedge your bets. Tie a selection of sizes in your chosen patterns – from indecently large right down to impossibly tiny. One day you might find that a change from one extreme to the other will put a salmon on the bank for you.

BIBLIOGRAPHY

The fishing books I list below are not the only ones I have read, but are those to which I have referred for confirmation of an idea, or a detail of a half-remembered dressing. Some of them, over the years, have given me the greatest pleasure.

Buckland, J., *The Pocket Guide to Trout and Salmon Flies*, Mitchell Beazley, London, 1986.
Clegg, T., *Hair and Fur in Flydressing*, second edition, private printing, 1969.
Dawes, M., *The Fly Tiers' Manual*, Collins, London, 1985.
Falkus, H., *Salmon Fishing, A Practical Guide*, Witherby, London, 1984.
Flydresser, the Journal of the Fly Dressers' Guild.
Fulsher, K., and Krom, C., *Hair-wing Atlantic Salmon Flies*, Fly Tyer Inc, North Conway, New Hampshire, 1981.
Hardy, Sir A., *The Open Sea, The World of Plankton*, Collins New Naturalist Series, no. 34, Collins, London.
Malone, E. J., *Irish Trout and Salmon Flies*, Colin Smythe, Gerrards Cross, 1984.
Martin, Alexander, Pre-war tackle catalogues.
Muus, B. J., and Dahlstrom, P., *Collins Guide to the Sea Fishes of Britain and North-Western Europe*, Collins, London, 1985.
Oglesby, A., *Salmon*, Macdonald & Co., London, 1980.
Orvis Company, *Index of Orvis Fly Patterns*, USA and Stockbridge, 1978.
Perrault, K., *Perrault's Standard Dictionary of Fishing Flies*, Daniel, Saffron Walden, 1984.
Price, T., *Fly Patterns, An International Guide*, Ward Lock, London, 1986.
Stewart, T., *Two Hundred Popular Flies*, Ernest Benn, London, 1979.
Sutherland, D., *The Salmon Book*, Collins, London, 1982.
Taverner, E., and others, *Lonsdale Library Vol X*, 'Salmon Fishing', Seeley Service, London, 1931.
Trout and Salmon magazine, EMAP, monthly.

INDEX

Please note that numbers which appear in roman indicate page numbers; those in italics are pages on which colour illustrations appear.

190